"Just like Otto Kernberg's work itse
of his many contributions to theory,
ously integrative and wholly origini

Mark Sc

Neuropsychoanal
International Psychoanalytical Association, and Science
Director of the American Psychoanalytic Association.
Director of Neuropsychology at the Neuroscience Institute of
the University of Cape Town

"It might not be an exaggeration to refer to Otto Kernberg as a "living legend" in the worlds of psychoanalysis and psychiatry. Setting out to chronicle his awesome career would be a daunting challenge to anyone, but Yeomans, Diamond, and Caligor have done just that, and they have done it beautifully. As Kernberg's collaborators, they know his work well. With rare clarity, they walk us through the evolution of his thinking and his seminal contributions to our understanding of human behavior."

John M Oldham, MD, *Distinguished Emeritus Professor at*
Baylor College of Medicine

"This collection shows Otto Kernberg as the intellectual and clinical giant he was – *the* most important and deepest psychoanalytic thinker and innovator from North America but one deeply knowledgeable of psychoanalytic and psychiatric viewpoints across the globe. Kernberg became known for integrating diverse ideas and bringing psychoanalysis into psychiatry in a rigorous way. He did it from a profound grasp of the central tenets of clinical psychoanalysis: Freud's discovery that patients suffer from unconscious ideas experienced with other persons that create conflicts of ambivalence with which they cannot cope. A "must-read" for every aspiring psychiatrist and psychoanalyst."

David Tuckett, *Distinguished Fellow and Training*
Psychoanalyst at the British Psychoanalytic Society,
Emeritus Professor of Decision-Making at the University
College London (UCL), and lead author of Knowing What
Psychoanalysts Do and Doing What Psychoanalysts Know

"Otto Kernberg has arguably contributed more to clinical theory, research, and practice than any other living psychoanalyst. In this invaluable volume, his closest colleagues convey his ideas with the same candid, curious, open-minded attitude that has pervaded Kernberg's life and work. Although his own writing can be daunting to readers not well versed in psychoanalytic concepts, this lucid explication of Kernberg's major contributions comes across as accessibly as a well-composed song. It should be read by anyone interested in personality, psychotherapy, psychopathology, sociopolitical and cultural processes, human hatred, and transcendent love — that is, by all of us who care about our world and the people in it."

Nancy McWilliams, PhD, ABPP *is Visiting Professor Emerita at Rutgers University's Graduate School of Applied & Professional Psychology*

Otto Kernberg

In this book, Frank E. Yeomans, Diana Diamond, and Eve Caligor provide a systemic review of Otto Kernberg's multiple contributions to psychoanalysis, psychiatry, psychology, and our understanding of the mind and group behavior.

The book spans the full scope of Kernberg's career, both highlighting the diversity of topics on which his writings have shed light and emphasizing conceptual threads that link the different areas of his work. It accessibly follows the experiences that had an impact on the development of his thought and the increasingly strong impact his writing and thinking have had on psychoanalysis and related fields. The authors draw on their decades of working closely with Kernberg to offer a unique insight into his teaching and research, focusing on his work on borderline and narcissistic pathology and the fundamental conceptualization of personality disorders.

Including an overview of Kernberg's critique and expansion of traditional psychoanalytic training, as well as his role in developing transference-focused psychotherapy, this book is an invaluable guide to students, researchers, and analysts in practice and training looking to integrate Kernberg's ideas into their own clinical and theoretical work.

Frank E. Yeomans is Clinical Associate Professor of Psychiatry at the Weill Medical College of Cornell University, Director of Training at the Personality Disorders Institute of Weill-Cornell; Lecturer in Psychiatry at the Columbia University College of Physicians and Surgeons Center for Psychoanalytic Training and Research; and President of the International Society for Transference Focused Psychotherapy.

Diana Diamond is Professor Emerita in the Doctoral Program in Clinical Psychology at the City University of New York and Senior Fellow at the Personality Disorders Institute at Weill Cornell Medical College. She is also Adjunct Full Professor in the New York University Postdoctoral Program in Psychotherapy and Psychoanalysis and an honorary member of the American Psychoanalytic Association. Dr. Diamond has published extensively on personality disorders, attachment, and narcissism.

Eve Caligor is Clinical Professor of Psychiatry at the Columbia Vagelos College of Physicians and Surgeons and Director of the Psychotherapy Division at the Columbia University Center for Psychoanalytic Training and Research.

Routledge Introductions to Contemporary Psychoanalysis

Aner Govrin, Ph.D.
Series Editor
Tair Caspi, Ph.D.
Executive Editor
Yael Peri Herzovich, Ph.D.
Assistant Editor

"Routledge Introductions to Contemporary Psychoanalysis" is one of the prominent psychoanalytic publishing ventures of our day. It will comprise dozens of books that will serve as concise introductions dedicated to influential concepts, theories, leading figures, and techniques in psychoanalysis covering every important aspect of psychoanalysis.

The length of each book is fixed at 40,000 words.

The series' books are designed to be easily accessible to provide informative answers in various areas of psychoanalytic thought. Each book will provide updated ideas on topics relevant to contemporary psychoanalysis – from the unconscious and dreams, projective identification and eating disorders, through neuropsychoanalysis, colonialism, and spiritual-sensitive psychoanalysis. Books will also be dedicated to prominent figures in the field, such as Melanie Klein, Jacques Lacan, Sandor Ferenczi, Otto Kernberg, and Michael Eigen.

Not serving solely as an introduction for beginners, the purpose of the series is to offer compendiums of information on particular topics within different psychoanalytic schools. We ask authors to review a topic but also address the readers with their own personal views and contribution to the specific chosen field. Books will make intricate ideas comprehensible without compromising their complexity.

We aim to make contemporary psychoanalysis more accessible to both clinicians and the general educated public.

Aner Govrin – Editor

Erotic Transferences
A Contemporary Introduction
Andrea Celenza

Otto Kernberg
A Contemporary Introduction
Frank E. Yeomans, Diana Diamond, and Eve Caligor

For more information about this series, please visit: www.routledge.com/Routledge-Introductions-to-Contemporary-Psychoanalysis/book-series/ICP

Otto Kernberg

A Contemporary Introduction

Frank E. Yeomans,
Diana Diamond, and
Eve Caligor

Routledge
Taylor & Francis Group

LONDON AND NEW YORK

Designed cover image: Michal Heiman, Asylum 1855–2020,
The Sleeper (video, psychoanalytic sofa and Plate 34),
exhibition view, Herzliya Museum of Contemporary Art,
2017

First published 2025
by Routledge
4 Park Square, Milton Park, Abingdon, Oxon OX14 4RN

and by Routledge
605 Third Avenue, New York, NY 10158

Routledge is an imprint of the Taylor & Francis Group, an informa business

© 2025 Frank E. Yeomans, Diana Diamond, and Eve Caligor

British Library Cataloguing-in-Publication Data
A catalogue record for this book is available from the British Library

ISBN: 9780367513337 (hbk)
ISBN: 9780367513344 (pbk)
ISBN: 9781003053415 (ebk)

DOI: 10.4324/9781003053415

Typeset in Times New Roman
by codeMantra

Contents

Acknowledgments

We are grateful to our editor, Aner Govrin, for inviting us to write the book on Dr. Otto Kernberg for the Routledge "Contemporary Introductions" series on major psychoanalysts.

This book has given us the opportunity to communicate to our readers a sense of the breadth and depth of Kernberg's contributions to psychoanalysis and related fields. We hope we have communicated in this relatively brief text some of what we have had the good fortune to get to know through decades of close contact with the man who has been both mentor and colleague to us. Working closely with Otto Kernberg has provided the opportunity to experience the human qualities that are the bedrock of his life's work. While his writings on love and aggression, theory, technique, teaching, research, and society provide the reader with important insights with regard to what it is to be human, direct contact with Kernberg himself has put us in contact with the boundless generosity and genuine humility that are at the core of the author, scientist, clinician, and thinker.

In some ways, Otto Kernberg has always hovered between the position of insider and outsider, a position that has enriched his ability to expand the boundaries of our understanding. Related to that position, he has always demonstrated the willingness to change his views as the fields he works in provide more data on which to reflect. As an insatiable reader and aficionado of art and the humanities, he has been able to integrate thoughts and perceptions from many fields. A mildly frustrating quality of Otto Kernberg is his frequent reluctance to take full credit for his work, often bestowing credit to "the team" when an objective view might focus the credit on him. In any case, over the years, his "team" has expanded to include colleagues in dozens of countries who bear witness to the value of his thinking. We hope our writing this text expresses some measure of our gratitude to and appreciation of this man who has inspired us to look more deeply into ourselves and others to achieve a finer and more empathic understanding of the complexity of the human experience.

Preface

Spanning six decades, the work of Otto Kernberg has made essential contributions to both psychoanalysis and descriptive psychiatry. He has consistently contributed to advancing our understanding of psychoanalytic theory and technique and to providing a conceptualization of personality disorders that enhances our ability to understand them and to treat patients suffering from that major form of psychopathology. At the heart of his work is an interest in personality development, describing and assessing personality pathology, and treating personality disorders, with a focus on understanding personality in terms of psychological structure. His concept of Borderline Personality Organization preceded by 40 years the current trend in the Diagnostic and Statistical Manual of Mental Disorders 5th Edition and the International Classification of Diseases 11th Revision to move away from a categorical understanding of personality disorders to a dimensional one. He has developed an approach to the assessment of personality disorders that combines the elements of psychiatric diagnosis and psychoanalytic concepts. Another major area of interest has been the study of narcissistic personality and its vicissitudes. In addition, Kernberg's writings over the years provide a series of reflections on the nature of love relations and of mourning. Beyond these themes, but closely related to personality and personality disorders, is the question of the dynamics of large groups and organizations, and the impact of those dynamics on society and politics.

Beyond these broad categories of psychoanalytic theory and technique and personality and its disturbances, Kernberg has made major contributions to psychoanalytic education. He has written important critiques of the organization of psychoanalytic institutes and training and has advocated for the development of a coherent curriculum that combines clear exposition of theory with description of the systematic application of psychoanalytic techniques. His vision sees a core understanding of theory and technique as providing a foundation for analytically trained clinicians that can be applied to different psycho-analytic approaches: psychoanalysis proper, supportive psychoanalytic psychotherapy, and the form of exploratory psychoanalytic therapy developed by Kernberg and his colleagues known as "transference-focused psychotherapy (TFP)".

In writing about these and other topics, Kernberg has authored, co-authored, or edited 33 books; has authored 287 articles; and has co-authored 75 articles. At age 95 (at this writing), he continues to contribute to the psychoanalytic and psychiatric literature.

Chapter 1

A Brief Professional Biography

Dedicating one's life to better understanding the human experience through the lens of psychoanalysis stems from a multitude of influences. While not pretending to fully explain the motivations for Otto Kernberg's dedication to psychoanalysis, reviewing certain personal and historic events may be relevant to our understanding of Kernberg's choice of career and direction within it. Otto Kernberg describes a childhood in Vienna that was marked by his father's special love of the city. The senior Kernberg, a functionary in the Austrian interior ministry who had served in the Austro-Hungarian army in World War I and maintained a loyalty to the Hapsburg monarchy, took pleasure in introducing young Otto, an only child, to the beauty of the city. In this context, the Anschluss in March 1938 was a brutal intrusion into his world. At age nine, he remembers witnessing, as a part of the crowd, the throngs welcoming Hitler to Vienna and shouting "Sieg Heil!". He did not immediately understand the meaning of it, but, as he put it, "From one day to the next, my world fell apart" (personal communication, January 14, 2023). After a childhood free of antisemitism, he and his parents were subjected to insults, attacks, and degradation in public during the next 16 months. On the morning of July 16, 1939, his father told him they were leaving Austria that day; he was to pack whatever he could into a suitcase and tell no one about the plan. The family fled to Italy and then to Chile, where they were relieved to find a warm and supportive atmosphere.

Kernberg traces his initial interest in psychiatry to the influence of his maternal uncle, Dr. Manfred Sackel, the neuropsychiatrist who developed insulin shock treatment. On a more personal level, the experience of symptoms of eating disorder as a child contributed to curiosity

DOI: 10.4324/9781003053415-1

about emotions and the mind. He was hospitalized for that condition at age five. While not remembering the specifics of the experience, he left the hospital cured and happy. His mother, though not a professional, was interested in psychology and attended lectures by Alfred Adler and Helene Deutsch. Upon her son's discharge from the hospital, she arranged for him to have therapy with an Adlerian psychologist from age five to eight.

As an adolescent in Chile, he was impressed by the leader of a Jewish-German youth group who was a Jungian analyst and would give talks about psychoanalysis to the group. It is not surprising that Kernberg, who had wanted to be a physician since childhood, after an initial interest in gastroenterology, shifted to neurology and an interest in psychiatry in medical school. When he went on to psychiatry training at the University of Chile in Santiago, an important influence was Ignacio Matte Blanco, the co-founder of the Chilean Psychoanalytic Society whose career evolved from neurology to psychiatry and then to psychoanalysis, becoming a member of the British Middle Group. Influenced by Matte Blanco and by the Kleinian impact on psychoanalysis in Chile, Kernberg's initial orientation was, and to a large extent continues to be, Kleinian. However, Kernberg emphasized (personal communicaton, January 14, 2023) that he was always suspicious of dogma and sought to understand alternative approaches, a goal which motivated his travel to the United States in 1959. Before that turning point, Kernberg held a number of positions in Chile, some of them simultaneously. After completing his residency in psychiatry at the University of Chile in Santiago in 1957, he went on, between that year and 1961, to the following positions: Professor of Psychopathology and Professor of Mental Health at the National Health Service School of Social Work, Assistant Professor of Psychiatry at the University of Chile, and Professor of Mental Health and Professor of Psychological Diagnosis at the Catholic University School of Psychology.

Another important experience in Chile was meeting Paulina Fischer, who was two years behind him in medical school. They met in a leftist Zionist youth group. She approached him to learn about psychoanalysis. They married a month after Kernberg's graduation from medical school and had three children: Martin, Karen, and Adine. Dr. Paulina Kernberg became renowned for her own contributions to psychiatry and psychoanalysis in her role as a pioneer in diagnosing and treating personality disorders in children and adolescents long before it was permitted to make those diagnoses in that population by the official diagnostic system (APA, DSM). The two Kernbergs' works complemented each other, and they often worked and taught at the same institution until her death from cancer in 2006.

Kernberg emphasizes his "double identity" as a psychiatrist rooted in both classical German descriptive psychiatry and psychoanalysis. This "double identity" has continued throughout his career and has marked his ongoing efforts to link psychoanalysis to psychiatric diagnosis. An impact of Matte Blanco's mentorship was an interest in research, especially research of the relation between psychoanalysis and the central nervous system. As we will see, Kernberg's commitment to research has been a distinguishing feature of his position within psychoanalysis, a commitment that has included research on psychotherapy process and outcome, on diagnosis and, more recently, on the relation between psychotherapy and neurobiology.

Seeking more knowledge about American psychiatry and, ultimately, ego psychology, Kernberg travelled to the United States. His first experience there was in 1959–1960 as a Rockefeller Foundation Fellow at the Henry Phipps Clinic of the Johns Hopkins Hospital in Baltimore. While there, Kernberg studied with Jerome Frank, with a special interest in Frank's practice of psychoanalytic group therapy. He also learned from psychiatrists at Chestnut Lodge. Contact with Harold Searles and Otto Will helped advance Kernberg's interest in applying psychoanalytic concepts and techniques to severely ill patients and to appreciate the central role of relationships, in particular the therapist-patient relationship, and the importance of the counter-transference in the therapeutic process.

After a brief return to Chile, the Kernbergs moved to the Menninger Foundation in Topeka, Kansas, which at that time was the bastion of American psychiatry. It is hard to overstate the importance of the Menninger Foundation in American psychiatry in the middle of the 20th century. In addition to the Menninger brothers, prominent staff and faculty during Kernberg's time there included Robert Wallerstein, Ernst and Gertrude Ticho, Herbert Schlesinger, Ann Appelbaum, Philip Holzman, and, a bit later, Glen Gabbard. Kernberg's Menninger years, from 1961 to 1973, were formative in his professional development and involved moving up the ranks from staff psychiatrist to eventually becoming the Medical Director (1969–1973) of the C.F. Menninger Memorial Hospital. As was the case with many psychiatrists at Menninger, he was also part of the Topeka Psychoanalytic Society, where he was a training analyst. During this period, he became involved with the American Psychoanalytic Association, serving initially on the Board of Professional Standards and on the Committee on Liaison with Latin American Colleagues.

The Menninger Foundation was known for promoting the biopsychosocial approach to treatment, combining psychoanalytically oriented individual therapy with a milieu treatment that was also based on psychoanalytic principles. A critical article underlying the milieu treatment was Thomas Main's "The Ailment" (1957). Some of Kernberg's early writings (1975b) as well as more recent writings (2023) have dealt with the use of the hospital setting as a therapeutic community, a concept he emphasized when he was Professor of Psychiatry at the Columbia University College of Physicians and Surgeons and Director of General Clinical Service at the New York State Psychiatric Institute (1973–1976) and then Medical Director of the New York Hospital – Weill Cornell Medical Center, Westchester Division (1976–1995).

Ego psychology was the psychoanalytic model that informed the treatment at Menninger's. Kernberg was most influenced there by Robert Wallerstein, who was the head of the research program, Ernst Ticho, whose broadmindedness and interest in new ideas Kernberg especially appreciated, and John Sutherland, the Director of the Tavistock Clinic and analysand of Ronald Fairbairn, who visited the Menninger Foundation regularly from London. The Menninger Psychotherapy Research Project, headed by Wallerstein, had an important impact on Kernberg's career, as will be discussed in more detail in Chapter 5.

During the Menninger years, as he became more familiar with psychoanalysis in the United States, Kernberg was interested in the work of ego psycholgists Hans Loewald, Otto Fenichel, and Paul Gray. In his work at Menninger, his attention was drawn to the need to understand those patients whose pathology presented in the broad area between neurosis and psychosis described by Rapaport, Schafer, and Knight (Knight, 1953). Kernberg found little to object to in ego psychology as far as it went but felt it did not provide an adequate conceptual basis for understanding many of the challenging patients at the Menninger Foundation. He saw these patients' generalized ego weakness, characterized by lack of impulse control, lack of anxiety tolerance, and troubled interpersonal relations, the primitive nature of their defensive organization, the infiltration of aggression into behaviors, and especially the lack of integrated identity, as incompatible with Freud's tripartite model of the mind that was central to ego psychology. In developing the broad concept of Borderline Personality Organization

(BPO; Kernberg, 1975), Kernberg turned to Klein's concept of the split, paranoid-schizoid psychological organization to better understand the psychological structure underlying serious personality pathology. He found concepts in Klein's *Envy and Gratitude* (1957) central in conceptualizing what he was seeing in his patients: the internalization and unconscious elaboration of early experiences of satisfaction/pleasure or pain/anger-hatred. These internalizations were associated with mental representations of an all-good other connected to a perfectly satisfied self and of an all-bad other associated with a suffering self. The lack of integration of these polarized internal representations did not seem compatible with Freud's tripartite structure. Kernberg understood the activation of these primitive internal representations as the basis the extreme shifts in affect states and tenuous hold on reality he observed in these patients in whom images from their internal world often prevailed over a more objective perception of reality.

Herman Van der Waals, a senior colleague at Menninger's, encouraged Kernberg's interest in narcissistic pathology. Kernberg's reflection on narcissism was enriched by dialogue with Herbert Rosenfeld, especially with regard to the role of aggression in the dynamics and structure of narcissistic personality. Betty Joseph was another important influence over time, with her emphasis on the need to focus on the interaction between patient and therapist and on countertransference in addition to attending to the content of the patient's discourse (Joseph, 1985).

A major focus of Kernberg's work has always been an emphasis on connecting our theoretical understandings with a corresponding systematic application of psychoanalytic techniques. For example, in contrast to the traditional Kleinian approach which focuses exclusively on exploration of intrapsychic reality, Kernberg's position is that work with more severely disturbed patients necessitates a dual focus that combines exploration of the patient's intrapsychic reality with attention to what is going on in the patient's life outside the sessions since so many of these patients act out their internal conflicts in the way they lead their lives and may engage in the process of free association in sessions in a way that leaves out and defends against split-off conflictual material. Kernberg developed sophisticated ways of using the treatment contract and frame, setting limits, choosing the material around which to intervene, and appropriately maintaining while sometimes deviating from technical neutrality. These were elaborations of psychoanalytic technique that we will discuss more fully in Chapter 4.

Kernberg's Menninger years included a three-month fellowship in Paris, an experience that had a strong impact on him and led to a life-long relation with André Green. Over the years, he appreciated Green's role as a bridge between the psychoanalytic mainstream, particularly the Kleinian elements, and the writings and influence of Jacques Lacan, a figure who Kernberg appreciated but criticized for his lack of attention to affect in the psychoanalytic process.

At the beginning of his prolific writing career, Kernberg's earli-est publications included articles on hysteria, neurotic depression, and anxiety neurosis (1959a, 1959b, 1959c). A next group of writings reflected the increased focus on both object relations and the role of research that would become central to his thinking: "Three Methods of Research on Psychoanalytic Treatment" (1965), "Structural Deriva-tives of Object Relationships" (1966), and, introducing what was to become a central theme throughout his career, "Borderline Personality Organization" (1967). The ensuing years brought many publications that built on his central themes (personality disorders, object rela-tions theory, psychoanalytic practice and education, narcissism, and love relations) and introduced new themes as his voracious reading and curiosity about the mind and the human experience encompassed developments in psychiatry and neurobiology, some of which will be mentioned below.

After his 14 years at Menninger, Kernberg described a certain rest-lessness and also the feeling that there was more to learn elsewhere. In addition, he experienced a level of tension in the analytic community that he said exceeded the kind of tensions that exist between those with different perspectives currently. There was an increasing feel-ing at Menninger that he was "the closet Kleinian"; when Anna Freud visited, he felt she looked askance at him (personal communication, January 14, 2023). At the same time, Kleinian purists were wary of Kernberg because he incorporated some of Kleinian thinking without adopting the whole body. This "in-between" position has characterized Kernberg throughout his career. He has, to some extent, suffered from it, but this position has also been the basis for his most meaningful contributions and the richness and originality he brings to them.

As described above, Kernberg came to New York in 1973 to run the psychiatric unit specializing in borderline pathology at the New York State Psychiatric Institute, affiliated with the Columbia University Col-lege of Physicians and Surgeons. He became a member of both the New York Psychoanalytic Society and Institute and the Columbia Center for

Psychoanalytic Training and Research, where he became a training and supervising analyst. Tensions led to his leaving the New York Institute after a year and becoming a central figure in the Columbia Center. Nevertheless, some of his most important professional relationships were with Margaret Mahler and Edith Jacobson, who were affiliated with the New York Psychoanalytic. Important collegial relations at Columbia Psychoanalytic included Robert Michels, Arnold Cooper, Michael Stone, Ethel Person, and Roy Schafer. The first four of these colleagues were also central faculty at the New York Hospital – Weill Cornell Medical Center, where Kernberg accepted the role of medical director of the Westchester Division of that hospital in 1976.

The position of medical director involved overseeing a 320-bed hospital that included acute, intermediate-stay, and long-term inpatients units, and an outpatient clinic. The inpatient units provided both general inpatient psychiatric care and also specialized treatments for child and adolescent patients, geriatric patients, substance abuse, eating disorders, psychosis, and borderline personality disorder. This richness of inpatient settings allowed for the further elaboration of forms of milieu treatments, rooted in the seminal work of Stanton and Schwartz (1954). Kernberg brought in talent from Menninger (Ann Appelbaum, Herbert Schlesinger), from Columbia (John Oldham, Michael Stone), and from Yale (Richard Munich and Charlies Swenson, who was later to become a leader in dialectical behavioral therapy (DBT) after introducing it to one of the units treating borderline patients at the Westchester Division). Kernberg's openness to new developments related to borderline personality disorder was clear in his early interest in Marsha Linehan and DBT. Linehan spent a sabbatical semester at the Westchester Division in the late 1980s. Subsequently, the hospital opened the second DBT program in the country, after Linehan's program in Seattle. Kernberg proposed offering Linehan a faculty position at Cornell, although the leadership of the Department of Psychiatry did not follow through on that proposal.

The richness and specialization of inpatient treatments decreased with the onset of managed care in the 1990s, which forced the Westchester Division's long-term units to shift to acute care. With that development, Kernberg and his core colleagues worked on shifting to a "hospital-without-walls" model of treatment that brought the major elements of the inpatient treatment, such as the possibility of combining family therapy with individual therapy, to the outpatient setting. Applying Kernberg's ideas about inpatient and milieu treatment shifted to colleagues in Europe who continued to consult with Kernberg about their work with patients hospitalized on a long-term basis.

From the 1970s on, Kernberg embarked on the series of books, articles, and studies for which he is best known. Seminal works included *Borderline Conditions and Pathological Narcissism* (1975a), *Object Relations Theory and Clinical Psychoanalysis* (1976), *Internal World and External Reality* (1980), and *Severe Personality Disorders, Psychotherapeutic Strategies* (1984). In the 1970s, Kernberg participated in a number of conferences that contrasted his understanding of narcissistic pathology and its treatment with the revolutionary views of Heinz Kohut as the latter developed self-psychology. Kernberg found these encounters stimulating and rejected the idea of an intense rivalry, believing that others seemed more interested in opposing the two analysts than he was (personal communication, January 14, 2023). Whether those conferences represented a rivalry or not, they can be seen as representing an ongoing tension about the underlying structure of those with pathological narcissism: whether it involves investment in a pathological grandiose self structure that defends against unconscious attacks on the self, as Kernberg would have it, or an arrest at stages of infantile narcissism necessitating processes of mirroring and idealization (Kohut, 1971). This was part of a deepening controversy in the analytic world between those who put the accent on achieving cognitive understanding of internal states, sometimes with an emphasis on deficits in psychological development (self-psychology, the relational school, mentalization based therapy), and those who emphasize the role of resolving conflicts among primitive unconscious affects and drives as the core of treatment (Klein, Kernberg), reflecting different understandings of human nature. Kernberg's view of human nature includes a keen awareness of, and guarded optimism with regard to, aggression:

> Concern... involves awareness of the serious nature of destructive and self-destructive impulses in the patient, the potential development of such impulses in the analyst, and the awareness of the limitation necessarily inherent in his or her therapeutic efforts with the patient....one might say that [the analyst's] concern involves the recognition of the seriousness of destructiveness and self-destructiveness of human beings in general and the hope, but not the certainty, that the fight against these tendencies may be successful....
>
> (Kernberg, 1975, p. 63)

In a way that set him apart from many analysts at the time, Kernberg understood the role of research in both developing psychoanalysis and defending it. Early in his tenure at the Westchester Division, Kernberg initiated a crucial working relationship with John Clarkin, PhD, the Director of the Cornell Department of Psychology in Psychiatry who, though trained mostly in cognitive behavioral psychology, was drawn to Kernberg's theory and treatment model. The fruitful collaboration between the two has continued for more than 40 years and was central in establishing the evidence base for transference-focused psychotherapy (TFP). This development will be discussed in more detail in Chapter 4. John Oldham joined John Clarkin in co-leading an informal Borderline Study Group at the Westchester Division that began to meet in the early 1980s. Other members of the original group included Ann Appelbaum, Steven Bauer, Arthur Carr, Paulina Kernberg, Harold Koenigsberg, Lawrence Rockland, Michael Selzer, Michael Stone, and Frank Yeomans. This group was the precursor of the Personality Disorders Institute (PDI) described below.

As Kernberg's writings attracted more attention, his national and international teaching increased. The traditional practice of giving lectures in different places shifted to developing ongoing relations with colleagues who formed satellite groups devoted to teaching and practicing his evolving model of therapy. An early example was his involvement in the Lindau Psychotherapie Wöchen, elaborate yearly meetings organized in Germany by Peter Buchheim and Manfred Cierpka who brought together an international array of lecturers and students. The collaboration with Buchheim and others led to the creation of a group of followers in Munich. Similar groups developed in Berlin and Vienna and then in Québec and in the Netherlands. The number of groups in different countries continued to grow and in 2012 the groups were formally linked by the creation of the International Society for Transference-Focused Psychotherapy (ISTFP) under the guidance of Dr. Stephan Doering in Vienna. As of this writing, the ISTFP includes members from thirty-six countries.

While Kernberg's years as director of a large psychiatric hospital required a major investment of time in the administrative and clinical activities of the hospital, Kernberg continued to produce a prodigious number of writings on psychoanalysis and related topics. He deepened his reflection on themes such as intrapsychic structure and structural change, classification of personality disorders, object relations and character analysis, narcissism, love relations, sexual desire, aggression, affect theory and drives, and psychoanalytic education. In this period, he increasingly addressed additional themes, such as groups and organizations, leadership, and group regression. The latter work was largely rooted in Bion's writings.

In 1989, he and his co-authors from the Borderline Study Group published *Psychodynamic Psychotherapy of Borderline Patients* (Kernberg et al., 1989), the first book articulating the modified psychoanalytic psychotherapy for borderline personality disorder that was later to become TFP, which has played an important role both in treating patients with borderline pathology and in establishing an evidence base for a psychoanalytic psychotherapy. Another important early text that came out of this group was Lawrence Rockland's book on supportive psychodynamic therapy for BPD patients (Rockland, 1992).

When Kernberg's long tenure as Medical Director of the Westchester Division and Vice Chair of the Department of Psychiatry ended in 1995, Jack Barchas, MD, the Chair of the Department of Psychiatry at the Weill Cornell Medical College, created the position of Director of the Personality Disorders Institute (PDI) for him. This new position provided the opportunity to increase his investigation of aspects of psychoanalysis, psychoanalytic psychotherapy, personality disorders, and the application of the former to the latter during a time when the fields of psychiatry and psychology were, respectively, increasingly focusing on biological aspects of psychiatry and cognitive behavioral therapies.

The PDI brought together Weill Cornell-Westchester, Columbia, and other faculty who were dedicated to working with and studying patients with personality disorders: John Clarkin, who was named Co-Director; Frank Yeomans, Director of Training; Eve Caligor; Monica Carsky; Jill Delaney; Diana Diamond; Pamela Foelsch; Catherine Haran; Perry Hoffman; James Hull; and Paulina Kernberg; Mark Lenzenweger; Lina Normandin; Michael Stone. While most members of the group shared a psychodynamic perspective, Dr. Hoffman was an early adherent to DBT. The PDI provided training to several psychology fellows who later became very involved in its research and training activities, including Kenneth Levy, Eric Fertuck, Barry Stern, Kevin Meehan, and Nicole Cain. Over the years, the PDI welcomed a great number of students from many countries as visiting fellows. Many of them went on to establish TFP groups in their home countries.

In keeping with his passionate interest in the state and future of psychoanalysis, Kernberg served as President of International Psychoanalytic Association (IPA) from 1997 to 2001. He accomplished numerous goals in that role. Chief among them was helping bring psychoanalysis into the broader scientific world in order to decrease a precarious isolation and insularity that had developed. He achieved success in this by encouraging the IPA to bring in excluded groups, especially psychologists with training in research, and to expand on Joseph Sandler's idea of research training and the development of research in psychoanalysis. Additional goals were to increase the links between psychoanalysis and psychiatry and the social sciences. His goal of including the teaching of psychoanalytic psychotherapy in institutes' curricula was not well received at the time but subsequently has gained momentum.

Kernberg's writings continued to reflect his energetic study of other areas within psychiatry and mental health, including keeping abreast of developments in the neurosciences. He engaged in active dialogues with Gerhard Roth, Jaak Panksepp, and Mark Solms. He continues to address the need he perceives for psychoanalysis to refine its understanding of drives and of the dynamic unconscious, especially from the perspective of affect theory (Kernberg, 2023). In addressing the issues of drives, he returns to the challenge of understanding the death drive/aggression. As elaborated in Chapter 2, Kernberg makes clear that he does not propose replacing Freud's dual concept of drives but rather proposes understanding drives as the result of primary affective motivational systems, as increasingly understood by studies in neurobiology (Roth and Strüber, 2014; Northoff et al., 2016; Kernberg, 2018).

Kernberg's recent writings reflect an increase in his concern about political and social developments. As described in Chapter 7, recent writings have included reviewing and extending psychoanalytic contributions to the understanding of the behavior of social masses in times of crisis, amplifying his earlier papers on the historical conditions that lead to sanctioned social violence towards outgroups. The final chapter of his most recent book (Kernberg, 2023) summarizes earlier contributions by Freud, Bion, Turquet, and Volkan and adds his analysis of the pathological interaction between traumatized masses and charismatic political leaders presenting with the personality structure Kernberg defined as malignant narcissism. In reflecting on similarities between some current developments in the United States and elsewhere in the world and those that characterized the Austria-Germany that he had to flee in 1939, Kernberg emphasizes the essential role of those elements in society that are needed to withstand the threat of totalitarianism: an independent judicial system, armed forces committed to constitutional law, open media, responsible religious organizations, a financial elite committed to the society, and effective governmental bureaucratic organizations, in addition to a strong sense of the traditional values that have defined society. In further reflecting on the latter, he expresses a cautionary note about an excessive movement towards a multiculturalism that fosters the existence of sharply different subcultures without adequate attention to the overarching principles and values that form the core of a society's identity.

In 2022, Kernberg retired from the professorship he held at the Weill Cornell Medical College since 1976. He moved with his wife and colleague, Dr. Catherine Haran, to an island off Maine, where he continues to write and to teach, supervise, and practice, mostly online. In this book, we will expand on the main thrusts of Kernberg's work as he continues to contribute to our understanding of the human experience and its vicissitudes. He writes as both a psychiatrist and a psychoanalyst trying to help us increase our understanding of our patients and how best to help them and as a scientifically and philosophically minded thinker trying to help us better appreciate the complexity of the human experience, with an overarching interest in identity as it integrates the brain, the mind, culture, and society.

Chapter 2

An Integrative Psychoanalytic Model of the Mind

Introduction

Otto Kernberg's extensive publications have addressed topics ranging from psychopathology to group psychology and from psychoanalytic technique to the nature of love relations. He has explored, in depth, psychoanalytic and psychotherapeutic approaches to personality pathology, and his model of psychoanalytic diagnosis and assessment can be seen as having charted a course for seminal developments in contemporary psychiatric nosology of personality disorders. In this book, we introduce the reader to many of Kernberg's most important and influential contributions.

At the core of Kernberg's wide-ranging contributions is his model of the mind and mental functioning (Kernberg, 1975a, 1976, 1980, 1984, 1992, 2004a, 2004b, 2012, 2018; Kernberg and Caligor, 2005). This model provides a basic frame of reference that is a constant thread running through his reflections on metapsychology, psychopathology, social theory, and most centrally, clinical work, as developed and elaborated over many decades. Kernberg's frame of reference is fundamentally psychoanalytic, and his model is intrapsychic in its orientation, focusing on how the internal world organizes subjective experience and behavior. His model of the mind emerges from his extensive experience treating a broad range of patients in deeper treatments over time and is intimately connected to clinical data. At the same time, he has consistently attended to empirical data and new knowledge emerging in adjacent fields, including neuroscience, developmental biology, the empirical study of psychopathology, attachment theory, and the social sciences, modifying his theories to accommodate ongoing scientific developments.

DOI: 10.4324/9781003053415-2

Kernberg (2004a, p. 47) describes his model as combining elements from ego psychology and object relations theory, two psychoanalytic frames of reference that have often been viewed as fundamentally incompatible. He draws upon Freud's dual drive theory and structural model of the mind along with the developmental models of the American ego psychologists Edith Jacobson, Margaret Mahler, and the culturalist Erik Erikson. Kernberg combines aspects of these models with contributions from the object relations theory school, focusing, in particular, on the theories of Melanie Klein and Ronald Fairbairn. Building on elements taken from these disparate models, while declining to adopt the fundamentals of any of them in their entirety, Kernberg creates a comprehensive, object relations theory-based model of mental functioning, pathology, and clinical change that is simultaneously integrative and wholly original.

Object Relations Theory and Internal Object Relations: Internal World and External Reality

Defining Internal Object Relations and Object Relations Theory

Kernberg adopts the approach of biological systems theory, in which lower order systems, often referred to as *structures*, are combined to form higher order systems. A *psychological* structure can be defined as an organization of related mental processes that is relatively stable and enduring over time. Psychological structures organize an individual's behavior and subjective experience.

Within Kernberg's model, "internal object relations" are the most basic psychological structures and the substructures that form the building blocks of the higher order structures that organize mental life (Kernberg, 1980, 2004a, 2012; Kernberg and Caligor, 2005). An internal object relation is a mental representation of a relationship, consisting of an image of the self (referred to as a self-representation) interacting with the image of another person (referred to as an object representation) and linked to a particular affect state. For example, one might imagine the image of a small, helpless self in relation to a powerful, threatening authority figure associated with feelings of fear, or a well-taken care of self in relation to a powerful and benign caretaker linked to feelings of safety. Each individual has a characteristic array of internal object relations that exist within their mind as latent structures. Specific internal object relations will be activated and enacted in different contexts and will color the individual's experience of that setting. In this process, an internal object relation, an internal structure that resides within the mind of the individual, is actualized in the form of the individual's emotional experience and behavior. For example, the fearful object relation just described might be activated in the context of interactions with authority figures, leading the individual to feel automatically disempowered and threatened in relation to authority. Alternatively, activation of the object relation of a benign caretaker in relation to a well-taken care of self will lead the individual to anticipate feeling gratified and safe in the setting of a dependent relationship. The designation "Object Relations Theory" is applied to those psychoanalytic models that place object relations at the center of mental life (Auchincloss and Samberg, 2012). Within Kernberg's model, internal object relations are the building blocks of mental life and related behavioral patterns, organizing motivational systems, defensive operations, and internalized values, as well as the subjective experience of self in relation to others.

Origins of Internal Object Relations

For Kernberg, affects are the inborn, biological drivers of human motivation, and internal object relations, derived from the interplay of affects and interactions with caretakers, serve as the basic building blocks of psychological motivational systems (Kernberg, 1976, 1984, 1992, 2004a, 2012). Employing a developmental model, Kernberg suggests that internal object relations are derived from the internalization of early interactions with caretakers as they are linked to inborn affect dispositions; psychological development is conceptualized as a process that integrates inborn, temperamental dispositions with developmental experience.

From birth onward, inborn affect dispositions are activated in relation to, regulated by, and cognitively linked to interactions with caretakers. When a high intensity affect is repeatedly experienced in the context of a particular kind of interaction, affective memories are organized to form the enduring, affectively charged representations or memory structures that constitute internal object relations. Kernberg emphasizes that what is internalized is not an image or representation of the other ("the object") but rather the relationship between the self and the other.

Kernberg posits that internalizations derived from interactions associated with high affect activation have different characteristics from those derived from interactions under conditions of low affect activation (Kernberg, 2004a, 2012). Under conditions of low affect activation, reality-oriented, perception-controlled cognitive learning takes place, leading to the formation of differentiated, gradually evolving definitions of self and others. These definitions start out from the perception of bodily functions, the position of the self in space and time, and the permanent characteristics of others. As these perceptions are integrated and become more complex, and interactions with others are cognitively registered and evaluated, working models of the self in relation to others are established.

In contrast, interactions associated with high affect arousal lead to the establishment of specific affective memory structures, or internal object relations, framed by the nature of the interaction between a baby and a caretaker. The central importance of internal object relations lies in their function as the basis of a system of psychological motivation, directing efforts to approach, maintain, or increase the conditions that generate peak positive affect states and to decrease, avoid, and escape from conditions of peak negative affect states. Thus, internal object relations are psychological structures with motivational implications. For example, feelings of gratification, repeatedly experienced in the context of being fed, or cared for, may be internalized as a memory structure of an attentive parental figure in relation to a cared for self, associated with feelings of gratification; this structure will then be activated in the setting of hunger or needing care, coloring the subject's expectations and experience of that interaction, and motivating their to approach the caretaker when in need. In contrast, feelings of frustration, repeatedly experienced in the context of being fed, or cared for, may be internalized as a memory structure of a teasing or even sadistic parental figure, associated with feelings of frustration or rage; this structure may be activated in the setting of hunger or needing care, coloring subject's expectations and experience of dependency, and motivating their to avoid the other when in need.

In Kernberg's model, internal object relations have a complex relationship to their developmental origins, reflecting a combination of actual and fantasied interactions with others as well as defenses in relation to both, all colored by the impact of inborn affect dispositions (Kernberg and Caligor, 2005). Thus, the fearful image of a small, terrified self in relation to a powerful, threatening authority may reflect an actual developmental experience, but could equally well reflect a young child's developmentally distorted view of parental authority or a defensively colored experience reflecting the projection of the child's hostile aggression onto an authority figure. We would add that these distortions will be especially prominent in the child with a high loading of constitutional aggression, reflecting the impact of temperamental factors on the development of internal object relations. As is the case with the negative experience, the gratifying image of an attentive care-taker in relation to the self may reflect actual experiences of care but could equally well reflect wishes and defenses in relation to parental neglect. In sum, past interactions with significant others, colored by fantasy, defense, and inborn affect dispositions, lead to the building up of the internal world; in turn, the internal world, derived from internali-zation of past relationships, organizes current experience and behavior. The constant interplay between the internal world and the external re-ality begins at birth and continues throughout the life cycle.

Moving towards Higher Levels of Integration: A Developmental Model

In Kernberg's model of the mind, internal object relations are not only the most basic psychological structures, but they also serve as the build-ing blocks of higher order structures, notably motivational systems, defensive operations, internalized values, and identity. Kernberg elabo-rates the relationship between internal object relations and higher order structures in terms of a series of successive steps involving progres-sive levels of integration and hierarchical organization of component structures (Kernberg, 1980, 2004a, 2012; Kernberg and Caligor, 2005). While these steps represent a hypothesized, but yet to be validated, de-velopmental model, they correspond closely with clinical observations emerging from the psychodynamic treatments of patients with a wide range of psychopathology and the progressive integration of psycholog-ical structures that can be seen to emerge during successful treatment.

Internal Object Relations and Splitting

As we've seen, internal object relations are memory structures internal-ized under peak affect activation, both positive and negative, and they function as a primary psychological motivational system, directing ef-forts to approach, maintain, or increase the conditions that generate peak positive affect states and to decrease, avoid, and escape from the conditions of peak negative affect states. In the early organization of these affective memory structures, those structures within the mind linked to positive affects are built up separately from those associated with negative affects. Thus, we see the separate development of two distinct sets of structures, those associated with positive affect, positive representations of both self and other, and affiliative behaviors, and those associated with negative affect, negative representations of both self and other, and aversive behaviors. With time, positive and negatively charged affective experiences, initially separate based on their association with different affect systems in the developing brain, come to be actively, defensively, dissociated from one another. The result is the development of two major domains of psychological experience, both sectors distorted and extreme. An idealized, or "all-good", sector is characterized by purely positive representations of self and other associated with positive, affiliative, affect states. A persecutory or paranoid, or "all-bad" sector is characterized by purely negative representations of other and threatened representations of self, associated with negative, aggressive, affect states.

The active, defensive, dissociation of positive and negatively charged sectors of experience is referred to as *splitting*. Splitting creates and maintains an internal world of "all-good" and "all-bad" internal object relations, with the underlying motivation being to maintain an ideal domain of experience characterized by the gratifying and pleasurable relation between self and others, while escaping from the frightening, paranoid experiences of negative affect states. Thus, splitting of experience into "all-good" and "all-bad" sectors sequesters and protects the idealized experiences from "contamination" with bad ones, but at the expense of creating a polarized, extreme, highly affectively charged, and distorted view of internal and external reality.

Under conditions of splitting, both positive and negative sectors have full access to consciousness. In some cases, this may mean that they are consciously experienced ("I am furious"); in other cases, this may mean that they are experienced only through behavior action while simultaneously denied ("I can be seen to be glaring at my therapist while denying any awareness of hostile feelings or behavior"). Positive and negative sectors and associated views of self and other may be experienced sequentially by the individual but are not experienced at the same time. As a result, at any given moment, the mother/other and self will be experienced as either all good or all bad, but are never experienced as simultaneously having both good and bad parts; in the moment, the part becomes the whole. In this setting, representations of negatively charged, painful, and dangerous representations tend to be projected, leading to a paranoid orientation characterized by fear of painful and dangerous relationships with people in the environment. In the psychoanalytic literature, defensive operations based on splitting are sometimes referred to as "primitive defenses", and this level of organization, in which idealized and paranoid sectors of experience are segregated and paranoid views are projected, corresponds with Melanie Klein's paranoid-schizoid position (Klein, 1946).

Internal Object Relations and Psychological Integration

We have described a basic level of psychological organization in which affectively charged, highly motivated, idealized, and paranoid sectors of experience are actively ("defensively") dissociated from one another in an effort to protect the idealized sector. The next step in Kernberg's model of psychological development is a gradual evolution towards the integration of these two polarized sectors, with resolution of splitting. Kernberg (1976, 2012; Kernberg and Caligor, 2005) suggests that this process of integration is facilitated by the development of cognitive capacities and ongoing learning regarding realistic aspects of the interactions between self and others under circumstances of low affect activation, in conjunction with a predominance of positive over negative interactions with others in the environment. Under these circumstances, the gradual coalescence of positively and negatively colored sectors initiates a virtuous cycle in which the intensity of negative affects and persecutory experiences is transiently diminished as a result of integration with more positive relational experience, facilitating, in turn, further integration. During this stage of psychological development, the individual recognizes that the relational world is not in fact "split" and that the other at any moment is neither "all good" nor "all bad", but rather has both "good' and "bad" aspects. Simultaneously, the individual comes to recognize that they, themself also have both good and bad parts, which is to say, the "bad" parts are no longer as consistently split off and projected, and that her aggression has been directed towards an object that is not "only bad" but rather also has positive aspects. The capacity to maintain awareness of one's own internal "badness" while taking responsibility for it and experiencing guilt is a crucial step in relinquishing splitting and moving towards integration. Melanie Klein referred to this development as entering the "depressive position" (1975), in which one relinquishes splitting-based defenses in relation to images of self and other. This process entails taking responsibility for, rather than projecting, "bad", aggressive aspects of the self, while recognizing that the same mother who is the target of one's aggression as a source of frustration and fear is also the mother who is loved as a source of gratification. The term "depressive" in this context refers both to mourning of the possibility of finding an ideal object and to the experience of guilt and depression in relation to recognizing one's own internal badness and that one's aggression has been directed towards objects that have positive as well as negative aspects.

Internal Object Relations and Identity Consolidation

As we've outlined, as internal object relations and associated affect states become less polarized, affectively charged, and extreme, the individual is able to tolerate and organize an increasingly integrated view of self and other. It becomes possible to simultaneously tolerate awareness of both negative, aggressive motivations and positive, affiliative motivations within the self, and to entertain and ultimately sustain a comparably integrated view of the other. Kernberg suggests that these better integrated (neither "all-good" nor "all-bad"), more realistic, and affectively toned down representations of self in relation to other naturally coalesce in relation to one another and are organized to form a complex, multifaceted, and realistic self-concept and concept of others. These developments move the individual beyond the black and white, moment-to-moment, poorly contextualized experience associated with splitting to provide a view of self and other that includes a view of the self as potentially imbued with both positive and negative attributes and motivations and that is continuous across time. A parallel integration occurs in the representations of significant others. These developments correspond to the consolidation of normal identity and determine the capacity for experiencing stable, coherent, and ambivalent relationships with others, sometimes referred to as "whole" (in contrast to "part") or "total internalized object relations". In Chapter 3, we discuss the manifestations of normal and pathological identity formation, as we introduce Kernberg's diagnostic framework.

Kernberg (1980) emphasizes that it was Erik Erikson (1950, Chapter 2, 1956) who first formulated the concept of normal ego identity and pathological identity formation, which Erikson referred to as "identity diffusion", a term that Kernberg adopts to describe the internal world and external experience under the dominance of splitting. Erikson proposed that normal ego identity is derived, developmentally, from early internalizations of affectively invested representations of significant others. However, for Kernberg, it was the work of Edith Jacobson (1964) in the United States and the work of Ronald Fairbairn (1954) in Great Britain that pointed specifically to the dyadic nature (i.e., it is the image of the *relationship*, not simply of the other, that is internalized) of early internalizations, so essential to Kernberg's formulation. The stage of identity consolidation, corresponding with the integration and crystallization of the experience of self and others, is equivalent to the phase of "object constancy" described by Mahler (Mahler et al., 1975), characterized by the child's developing capacity to maintain a continuous and integrated (in terms of "bad" aspects being part of an overall, integrated, predominantly positive) mental representation of mother, even in the face of frustration and/or physical separation.

Defenses, Unconscious Motivational Structures, and Internalized Value Systems

In Kernberg's model, the achievement of identity consolidation, object constancy, and the depressive position coincide with additional changes in mental organization. Kernberg focuses, in particular, on the development of the capacity for repression, leading to the formation of an unconscious system of highly charged motivational structures and the formation of an integrated system of internalized values, all central to Freud's (1923/1961) structural model of the mind (Kernberg 1976, 2004a; Kernberg and Caligor, 2005).

Repression

The capacity to reject threatening, painful, or anxiety-provoking aspects of psychological experience and to automatically eliminate them from consciousness is referred to as "repression". Within the framework of Kernberg's formulation of object relations theory, development of the capacity for repression is closely linked to identity consolidation. As a multifaceted, conscious sense of self, reflecting the crystallization of an array of relatively well-integrated internal object relations, evolves, so too does the capacity to automatically split off object relations that are less well integrated and banish them from conscious self-experience. Thus, in the process of identity consolidation, some internal object relations, typically those most closely linked to conflictual aggressive, sexual and dependent motivations, may remain poorly integrated, extreme, and highly affectively charged. These highly motivated object relations are "conflictual" in that they are incompatible with the individual's overall sense of self. As a result, they are excluded from conscious self experience and banished from consciousness, that is, repressed.[1] Thus, within Kernberg's frame of reference, it is highly affectively charged, conflictual object relations, incompatible with the individual's dominant, self-experience that constitute "the repressed", or the "dynamic unconscious".

In sum, for Kernberg, emergence of the capacity for repression and formation of the dynamic unconscious coincides with identity consolidation; the capacity for repression both reflects and facilitates the progressive integration and organization of psychological structures. Where defensive operations based on splitting, involving mutual dissociation of positive and negative sectors of experience, interfere with the normal integration of these sectors, defenses based on repression ("neurotic defenses") do not interfere with the integration of persecutory and idealized sectors, and at the same time facilitate further integration by effectively eradicating from conscious awareness of those aspects of experience that are most conflictual.

Internal Object Relations and internalized Value Systems

In Kernberg's model, coinciding with identity formation, we see the organization of an integrated system of internalized morals and values, often referred to as the "superego". Following Jacobson (1964), Kernberg suggests that the superego is constituted by successive layers of internalized self and object representations (Jacobson, 1964; Kernberg, 1984) in a process in many ways analogous to the process of identity consolidation as he describes it. A first layer of negatively affectively charged, persecutory, split, representations reflects a demanding and prohibitive, primitive morality as experienced by the child in relation to environmental and parental prohibitions. A second, more advanced, layer of organization is constituted by ideal representations of self and others reflecting early childhood ideals that promise the assurance of love and dependency if the child lives up to them. The integration of the earliest, persecutory and the later, idealizing representations tones down and modulates the intensity of both. In this process, a new level of organization is introduced into the system of internalized values, corresponding with a decrease in the tendency to reproject these representations (i.e., the threat of internal disapproval replaces fear of disapproval or attack by others in guiding moral values and behavior). This level of organization also brings about the capacity for internalizing more realistic, toned-down, demands and prohibitions from the parental figures, leading to a third layer of integration of internalized value systems. This final stage corresponds also with the formation of normal identity, and integration and consolidation of the structures that comprise identity facilitate this parallel development in the system of internalized values.

Motivational Systems, the Dynamic Unconscious, and the Drives

For Kernberg, affects are the inborn, biological drivers of human motivation, and internal object relations, derived from the interplay of affects and interactions with caretakers, serve as the basic building blocks of psychological motivational systems (1976, 1984, 1992, 2012). Thus, from the start, biology and relational experiences coalesce in the formation of motivational systems. As psychological development leads to the progressive integration of idealized and persecutory internal object relations, affect dispositions become increasingly complex and well modulated. These relatively well-integrated structures, associated with relatively well-modulated affect dispositions, are organized to form conscious motivational systems. With identity formation, these motivational systems are further integrated and become part of normal identity and the mature system of internalized values. At the same time that we see the development of conscious motivational systems, as a result of constitutional and environmental factors a subgroup of internal object relations remains poorly integrated and highly affectively charged. As we've outlined, with the achievement of identity formation, object constancy, and the capacity for repression, these psychological structures and associated affect dispositions are not integrated into dominant self-experience, but rather are repressed. These repressed, "high affect" mental structures constitute the dynamic unconscious, and they serve as an unconscious motivational system, corresponding with extreme manifestations of sexual, aggressive, and dependent impulses, needs, and wishes. It is the internalized system of values, in conjunction with the dominant sense of self that crystallizes with identity formation, that is responsible for rejecting these highly charged and relatively poorly integrated mental structures from the conscious sense of self by way of repression.

We turn at this point to the central issue of the drives. In classical psychoanalysis, the "drives", aggression and libido, are viewed as the inborn source of human motivation and the source of all psychological conflict (Freud, 1923/1961). In contrast, for Kernberg, affects are the inborn components of motivational systems, and internal object relations, derived from the interplay of affects and interactions with caretakers, serve as the basic structures in the psychological development of motivational systems. Despite this fundamental divergence from the classical formulation of drive, Kernberg opts to retain the drive concept, viewing it as crucial to psychoanalytic understanding of human motivation, psychological conflict, and developments in treatment. Kernberg (1992, 2004b) suggests that rather than the most basic motivational systems, the drives, libido and aggression, represent the supraordinate organization of internal object relations related to peak positive or negative affect states, relegated to the dynamic unconscious. These object relations, at their highest level of organization, constitute the drives.

Conclusion

In this chapter, we have provided a brief introduction to Kernberg's model of the mind. This model is both integrative, employing contributions from a variety of psychoanalytic models of mental functioning, and coherent, referring back to internal object relations as forming the basic infrastructure of the mind. Within this frame of reference, affects are the primary inborn motivators of human experience and behavior. From birth onward, the interplay between affects and the relational world leads to the formation of internal object relations. These affectively charged, most basic structures can be seen to function as the building blocks for the higher order mental structures central to all psychoanalytic models of the mind including motivational systems, defenses, internalized values, and identity.

Note

1 It is important to distinguish between processes related to repression and those related to splitting. In the setting of repression, conflictual aspects of mental life organized as affectively charged internal object relations are stably excluded from an otherwise integrated self-experience and from consciousness. In splitting, in the absence of an integrated sense of self, idealized and paranoid internal object relations that are in conflict with one another are mutually dissociated but remain accessible to consciousness, just not at the same time.

Chapter 3

Focusing on Psychological Structures

Kernberg's Approach to Diagnosis and Classification of Personality Pathology

Introduction

One of Otto Kernberg's most influential contributions has been the introduction of an object relations theory (ORT)-based approach to diagnosis and classification of personality pathology. This diagnostic framework, often referred to as "structural diagnosis" or "level of personality organization" (Kernberg 1976, 1984, Kernberg and Caligor, 2005), builds on extensive clinical experience treating patients with a wide range of personality pathology and is embedded in Kernberg's ORT-based model of the mind and mental functioning (see Chapter 2). Structural diagnosis focuses on characterizing personality pathology, first, in terms of severity of impairment of personality functioning and, second, in terms of salient personality traits or personality style. Severity of pathology, in contrast to personality style or type of personality disorder, is understood to be the most powerful predictor of prognosis and clinical course (Crawford et al., 2011; Hopwood et al., 2011), and structural diagnosis can be used to guide psychodynamic treatment planning and to anticipate developments in treatment (Caligor et al., 2018; Clarkin et al., 2021). This diagnostic framework, focusing on severity of impairment of personality functioning to classify personality pathology, is mirrored in the Diagnostic and Statistical Manual of Mental Disorders, Fifth Edition (DSM-5) Alternative Model of Personality Disorders (American Psychiatric Association, 2013) and International Classification of Diseases, Eleventh Revision (ICD-11) (World Health Organization, 2019) classifications of personality disorders, both of which classify personality disorders dimensionally according to severity of pathology of self-functioning

DOI: 10.4324/9781003053415-3

and interpersonal functioning. All three of these models embrace the observation that the core, defining features characterizing all personality disorders are impairment of self-functioning and of relatedness with others.

A Model of Personality Focusing on Psychological Structures

Within the ORT model, personality functioning and pathology are understood as expressions of mental structures (see Chapter 2), where mental structures are the psychological processes underlying and organizing the descriptive features of personality functioning. Thus, rather than focusing on the descriptive features of personality functioning per se, for example, dominant traits or personality style, diagnosis within the ORT model focuses on the underlying processes that organize observable, descriptive features.

To better understand the use of the term "structure", consider the psychological structure identity. Identity is the structure, the network of psychological processes or functions that organize, collectively, the individual's sense of self, the experience of others, and the capacity for goal directedness. One can assess identity formation by evaluating its expression in these functions. Thus, while psychological structures are not directly observable (one cannot see "identity"), they are actualized in descriptive features of personality functioning.

Kernberg identifies six core mental structures central to personality functioning and personality disorders. As we've described, "identity" is the psychological structure that organizes the individual's experience of self and the experience of others in interaction and the capacity for goal-directedness (Kernberg, 2006). Identity consolidation distinguishes between normal personality and mild, subsyndromal impairment in personality functioning, on the one hand, and the more severe, personality disorders, on the other (Kernberg, 1984; Kernberg and Caligor, 2005). Along with identity, the ORT model focuses on "quality of object relations" (internal working models of relationships and interpersonal relations), "defensive operations" (customary ways of coping with external stress and internal conflict), "reality testing" (the capacity to distinguish between internal and external reality), "moral functioning" (ethical behavior, ideals, and values), and quality and modulation of "aggression" (Kernberg and Caligor, 2005).

Focusing on these structures, Kernberg's approach to personality disorders describes a continuous spectrum of personality functioning and pathology across the dimension of severity, spanning the normal personality to the most severe personality disorders. In the normal personality, (1) identity is fully consolidated, corresponding with a well-integrated, stable, and realistic sense of self and a corresponding sense of significant others, along with the capacity to identify and pursue long-term goals; (2) relations with others are marked by a capacity for concern, mutual dependency, and intimacy; (3) mature defenses predominate and allow for adaptation to life and flexible management of psychological conflict; (4) moral functioning is internalized, stable, and linked to personally and consistently held values and ideals; (5) reality testing is stable even in areas of conflict or in the setting of affect activation; and (6) aggression is well integrated and well modulated (Hörz et al., 2012; Caligor et al., 2018).

In contrast, with the introduction of personality pathology, we see deterioration – though sometimes uneven deterioration – in functioning in all these domains, progressively worsening as pathology becomes more severe. Thus, in the setting of personality disorders, (1) identity is poorly consolidated, reflected in an experience of self and others that is distorted, superficial, unstable, and highly affectively charged, and in an impaired capacity to identify and pursue long-term goals; (2) relations with others are superficial, often based on need fulfilment, and increasingly exploitive as pathology becomes more severe; (3) lower-level, splitting-based defenses predominate and maintain a dissociated, black-and-white quality of experience while introducing severe rigidity and poor adaptation into personality functioning; (4) moral functioning is inconsistent and, at the most severe end of the spectrum, is characterized by antisocial features and an absence of internalized values or ideals; and (5) reality testing is vulnerable in the setting of affect activation, psychological conflict, or interpersonal stressors; (6) aggression is not well modulated and is inappropriately expressed in relation to self and/or others (Hörz et al., 2012; Caligor et al., 2018).

Psychological Structures and Structural Diagnosis

Building on a structural approach to understanding personality, Kernberg's initial diagnostic formulation focused on distinguishing personality disorders from milder or subsyndromal personality difficulties, on the one hand, and from the more severe, psychotic disorders, on the other hand,. This initial classification emerged from recognition of the profound clinical implications of making these distinctions and of the need for assuring diagnostic clarity before initiating treatment. Specifically, individuals with milder pathology were found to do well in a wide variety of treatments, including unstructured psychotherapeutic treatments such as psychoanalytic psychotherapy and psychoanalysis. In contrast, those with personality disorders, while often benefitting from psychodynamic therapy, required a more structured treatment approach such as transference-focused psychotherapy (TFP) and tend to do poorly in less structured treatments. In contrast, those with psychotic illness were found to benefit from therapeutic efforts that focus on providing support as well as structure (Kernberg, 1976, 1984).

Kernberg defined these three general levels of severity by focusing on the core domains of identity, defenses, and reality testing, leading to what he referred to as a "structural diagnosis" corresponding with different levels of "personality organization". At the mildest level of severity is the neurotic level of personality organization (NPO), corresponding with subsyndromal personality pathology and characterized by consolidated identity, the predominance of repression-based and higher-level defenses, and intact and stable reality testing. These individuals tend to function well, with difficulties typically limited to focal domains of functioning (e.g., problems with intimacy or self-esteem). At the next level of severity is the borderline level of personality organization (BPO)[1] reflecting clinically significant personality pathology and characterizing all of the familiar, categorical, personality disorders described in DSM-5 and ICD-10. BPO is characterized by failure of identity consolidation, the predominance of splitting-based defenses and intact but vulnerable reality testing. Individuals organized at a BPO tend to have global impairment of self- and interpersonal functioning ranging from moderate to extreme severity. Finally, the third and most severe diagnostic group is the psychotic level of personality organization, corresponding with a subset of psychotic disorders that may superficially present as personality pathology, characterized by failure of identity consolidation, the predominance of splitting-based and psychotic-level defenses, and frank failure of reality testing.

Structural diagnosis was first formally introduced by Kernberg in the 1960s (1967, 1975a) and has been further developed during the ensuing decades based on an accumulation of clinical and empirical research on the evaluation and treatment of personality pathology.

Determination of identity formation, defenses, and reality testing is complemented by the description of quality of object relations, moral functioning, and quality of aggression to provide a fine-grained description of dominant features of personality functioning at different levels of severity. This approach allows clinicians to differentiate different levels of severity within the BPO range: high BPO (mild severity), middle BPO (moderate severity), and low BPO (extreme severity). Those with higher levels of severity have a poorer prognosis and require more highly structured treatments (Clarkin et al., 2021). This overall framework is outlined in Table 3.1.

In sum, characterization of the core psychological structures identity, defenses, quality of object relations, moral functioning, aggression, and reality testing enables the clinician to describe a patient's "personality organization", a dimensional assessment of personality disorder reflecting the severity of pathology and clinical prognosis (Kernberg, 1984; Kernberg and Caligor, 2005). Within this framework, patients can be described as having a normal personality organization, an NPO, a high BPO, a middle BPO, or a low BPO; these terms describe the trajectory from the healthiest to the most severe personality pathology.

Core Structural Domains of Personality Health and Pathology

Identity: The structural approach to personality pathology focuses, in particular, on identity, the psychological structure that organizes the experience of self and others in interaction and the capacity for goal-directedness. The construct of identity is the cornerstone of the ORT model of personality disorders, with pathology of identity formation being the hallmark of all of the syndromal personality disorders.

Normal identity formation is manifested in the ability to invest, over time, in professional, intellectual, interpersonal, and recreational interests, and to "know one's own mind" with regard to one's values, opinions, tastes, and beliefs. The coherent sense of self that is conferred by normal identity formation is basic to self-esteem, the capacity to make and derive pleasure from commitments to relationships and to work, and to pursue long-term goals. A coherent and integrated conception of others, in addition, is associated with the ability to accurately appreciate the internal experience of others, contributing to the capacity for empathy and social tact, and thus confers the ability to interact and relate successfully with others. Identity formation also has

Table 3.1 Structural Approach to the Nosology of Personality Pathology

	Normal Personality Organization	Neurotic Personality Organization	High Borderline Personality Organization	Middle Borderline Personality Organization	Low Borderline Personality Organization
Identity	Consolidated, with stable and integrated sense of self and others	Consolidated, with stable and integrated sense of self and others	Mild-moderate identity pathology with some instability and distortion in sense of self and others	Severe identity pathology with polarized and affectively charged, distorted, and unstable experience of self and others	Severe identity pathology with polarized and highly affectively charged, distorted, and unstable experience of self and others
Object Relations	Deep, mutual relations; capacity for concern	Deep, mutual relations; capacity for concern; some conflict	Some capacity for dependent relations; relations highly conflictual or distant	Relations are based on need-fulfillment; limited to no capacity for dependent relations	Relations based on frank exploitation; others are used as a means to an end; no capacity for dependency
Predominant Defensive Style	Mature and repression-based	Repression-based	Repression-based and splitting-based	Splitting-based	Splitting-based
Moral Functioning	Internalized, consistent, flexible	Internalized, consistent but rigid or demanding	Variable across individuals; may see marked rigidity combined with focal deficits	Moderate pathology; failure of internalized values; inconsistent or deficient moral functioning; may see circumscribed antisocial behaviors	Extreme pathology with absent or corrupt moral system; prominent antisocial traits with frank antisocial behavior

(Continued)

Table 3.1 (Continued)

	Normal Personality Organization	Neurotic Personality Organization	High Borderline Personality Organization	Middle Borderline Personality Organization	Low Borderline Personality Organization
Aggression	Modulated; appropriate	Modulated; inhibited	Verbal aggression; temper outbursts; self-directed aggression in the form of self-neglect	Poorly integrated and poorly modulated; potential for aggression against self and others; outbursts, threats, and self-injurious behavior	Severe aggression against self and others; assault, intimidation, and self-mutilation
Reality Testing	Intact and stable	Intact and stable	Intact Concrete thinking in areas of conflict	Vulnerable reality testing and concrete thinking in areas of conflict Altered mental states without loss of reality testing e.g., dissociation, depersonalization	Vulnerable reality testing and concrete thinking Altered mental states without loss of reality testing e.g., dissociation, depersonalization

bearing on the nature of affective experience; identity consolidation is associated with the capacity to experience a range of complex and well-modulated affects in the setting of the predominance of positive affective experience. Identity consolidation also confers the capacity to experience states of high affective arousal without the risk of loss of impulse control or compromise of reality testing, reflecting the role of a consistent and stable self in contextualizing and making sense of intense affect states.

In contrast, individuals with personality disorders, that is, those at a borderline level of personality organization, suffer from pathology of identity formation, reflected in the absence of a fully elaborated, stable, and coherent sense of self and others. Here, the sense of self and that of others are more or less unstable, distorted, extreme, discontinuous, and poorly contextualized. Failure of identity consolidation is also reflected in difficulty identifying and sustaining longer-term goals or to fully invest in relationships and personal interests. Tastes, opinions, and values are inconsistent, typically adopted from others in the environment, and may shift easily and dramatically with changes in milieu. In the setting of poorly consolidated identity, affective experience is superficial, poorly integrated, and predominantly negative, and in the setting of conflict, often extreme and poorly modulated. Identity diffusion is characterized by the predominance of negative affective experience, often in the form of chronic dysphoria, free floating anxiety, or feelings of emptiness, with limited capacity for enjoyment, pleasure, or contentment. Capacity for empathy and ability to mentalize is impaired.

Clinical Illustrations of Identity Pathology

A young woman with significant identity pathology (histrionic personality disorder with dependent features organized at a high BPO level of personality organization) who was seen in consultation had worked a series of jobs since graduating college; none had been particularly interesting or meaningful to her, and she couldn't think of anything she wanted to do. When the consultant asked her to describe herself, she could come up with little to say, but did comment that she felt chronically depressed, empty, and aimless, with the exception of those times she was dating a new man, when she felt "wonderful". She described how her view of herself and her mood state shifted, depending on whether or not there was a man in her life; a new romantic interest lifted her from dysphoria and self-loathing, and left her feeling "like a new person". She changed her style of dress, taste in music, and patterns of speech to suit her latest boyfriend. When asked about the important people in her life, she explained that boyfriends came and went; typically, they seemed great at first but quickly became controlling and abusive. Her descriptions of the other people in her life were polarized, vague, and general, for example, characterizing someone as "nice", "pretty", and "funny" or "selfish" and "heartless".

Another patient (narcissistic personality disorder (NPO) organized at a low BPO level of personality organization), seen in couples' therapy, was hostile and verbally abusive with his wife, but when socializing in other settings could be charming and funny. During the initial consultation in which he met with the consultant without his wife, the patient acknowledged having married his wife because of her substantial financial resources. When she had, over the years, raised the possibility of leaving the marriage, he had threatened to kidnap their young child. When asked to describe his wife, the patient could only provide a string of negative adjectives such as "rich bitch", "boring", "nagging", and "a fool", and explained that he had never derived any pleasure from their relationship beyond what she offered materially. When asked to describe himself, he acknowledged that most of the time he felt "better and smarter", but that this view of himself would at times collapse, leaving him feeling "like a worm".

While most clearly evident in the DSM-5 borderline personality disorder, some degree of identity pathology characterizes all syndromal personality disorders. There are different degrees of identity pathology and different ways in which identity pathology may become manifest. Borderline personality disorder is, in many ways, the prototype of the personality disorders characterized by identity disturbance; both sense of self and sense of others are polarized, vague, unrealistic, and unstable (Sharp et al., 2015). Temporal discontinuity tends to be an especially prominent subjective manifestation of identity pathology in this group. In contrast, in NPD a more stable sense of self, albeit distorted, not solidly based in reality, and often fragile, coexists with what is often a dramatically superficial, shadowy, or caricature-like experience of others, even in individuals who are highly intelligent and accomplished. Feelings of inauthenticity tend to be an especially prominent subjective manifestation of identity pathology in the narcissistic group when defenses fail. In the schizoid personality, in contrast, we see a capacity to appraise others in the absence of any integrated or stable sense of self, in conjunction with prominent feelings of emptiness.

In personality disorders falling in the high-level BPO range, identity disturbance can be relatively mild, characterized by a sense of self that is less unstable than that characteristic of individuals organized at a low borderline level, along with a better developed capacity to realistically experience and sustain relationships with significant others, albeit with limited capacity for intimacy and mutuality.

Defenses: Defenses are an individual's automatic psychological response to external stressors or psychological conflict. They exist on a spectrum, from most to least adaptive (Vaillant, 1994). At the most adaptive and flexible end of the spectrum are the mature or healthy defenses. These are followed by the repression-based defenses, which introduce rigidity into personality functioning while stably keeping out of consciousness aspects of self-experience that are conflictual, incompatible with the subject's dominant sense of self. Next are the highly maladaptive splitting-based, or image-distorting, defenses. As discussed in Chapter 2, it is the predominance of splitting-based defenses that maintain the poorly integrated polarized nature of experience of self and others in those disorders characterized by failure of identity consolidation. Splitting-based defenses function to segregate idealized, positively valanced sectors of experience and associated object relations, from persecutory, negatively valenced sectors. This division is thought to be motivated by the need to prevent the contamination or destruction of ideal object relations by aggressively infiltrated ones. Splitting-based defenses lead to black-and-white thinking in which experiences of self and other are either all-good and idealized (the best, most attentive caretaker and the perfectly gratified self, linked to feelings of bliss) or paranoid and devalued (the callous, neglectful caretaker and the frustrated, helpless self, linked to feelings of rage). Splitting-based defenses result in distortions in the experience of self and other (as a result are sometimes referred to as "image-distorting defenses"), are highly maladaptive, and introduce severe rigidity into personality functioning. At the most pathological end of the spectrum and most maladaptive are the psychotic defenses, which are associated with frank loss of reality testing.

Quality of object relations: It refers to one's "internal working models of relationships", the internal beliefs, expectations, and capacities that organize interpersonal relations. It is reflected in the nature of an individual's interpersonal relations and their expectations of what they get out of and give to important relationships. In the normal personality, we see object relations in depth – the ability to maintain relationships that are based on an understanding of give and take, to appreciate and care about the needs of the other independent of the needs of the self, and a capacity for mutual dependence and concern. In contrast, personality disorders are associated with significant pathology of object relations, which are predominantly need-fulfilling in orientation and deteriorate with increasing severity of pathology to become frankly exploitative.

Moral values: The normal personality is associated with a commitment to values and ideals and a "moral compass" that is consistent, flexible, fully internalized (i.e., one plays by the rules even when no one is watching), and fully integrated into the individual's sense of self. In the neurotic personality, moral values and ideals are also consistent and fully internalized but may be excessively rigid. In contrast, personality disorders are characterized by a variable but clinically significant degree of pathology in moral functioning, ranging from mild to extreme impairment. At the most severe end of the spectrum, we see the absence of any internal moral compass and a lack of capacity for guilt or remorse, characteristic of patients functioning at a low BPO level, and in particular those with antisocial personality disorder or severe narcissistic pathology with antisocial traits.

Aggression: In the normal personality, aggression is well modulated and well integrated, and is manifest in appropriate and measured expressions of anger as well as in positive derivatives such as self-assertion and competition. In the neurotic personality organization, aggression is also typically well modulated and integrated, though the individual may demonstrate inhibitions in normal expressions of aggression or brief, relatively well-controlled flares of temper. In contrast, in the personality disorders, difficulty managing aggression is central to psychological functioning. This is especially pronounced in the severe personality disorders where intense affects such as rage, hatred, and envy often predominate. Aggression may be directed towards others in the form of verbal outbursts or threat, and in severe cases, physical violence and sadism, and/or directed towards the self in the form of self-injurious behaviors, risk-taking, self-neglect, or self-mutilation.

Reality testing and reflective capacities: Within a psychoanalytic frame of reference, reality testing refers to the capacity to differentiate self from nonself, to distinguish intrapsychic from external sources of stimuli, and to maintain empathy with ordinary social criteria of reality. All of these functions are typically lost in the psychoses, and they are manifested particularly in hallucinations and delusions (Kernberg,

1976, 1984). Sustained loss of perceptual reality testing is not a feature of personality disorders. However, transient loss of reality testing can be seen in some of the more severe personality disorders, especially in the setting of alcohol and substance misuse. Personality disorders may also be associated with disturbances in the sense of reality without frank loss of reality testing, such as dissociation, derealization, and depersonalization. In addition, in the setting of interpersonal conflict, individuals with severe personality disorders are vulnerable to highly concrete, though not frankly psychotic, mental states. Here the individual's experience in the moment leaves little room for entertaining alternative perspectives ("How I see it is how it is") or to reflect upon what might be happening. An internal OR dyad is activated in which the internal representations of self and other predominate over a more objectively accurate appraisal of the interaction. For example, a 29-year-old woman with borderline personality disorder presented with unstable relationships with men, while noting that many of her breakups were precipitated by her conviction in the moment that her boyfriend was lying to her – in her mind, he was an untrustworthy, exploitative liar. These episodes, though very dramatic, were time limited, often followed by frantic attempts to reestablish the relationship. In personality disorders, as a rule, thinking tends to be more concrete in areas of conflict and interpersonal intensity. As pathology becomes more severe, so, too, does the vulnerability to concrete thinking, reflecting the impact of internal representations on the experience of external reality, with a parallel decline in the capacity to reflect upon internal states in self and other (i.e., the capacity to mentalize).

From early in his writings, Kernberg understood the shared structure underlying personality pathology and the wisdom in focusing on structural elements in treating personality disorders. Nevertheless, the structural understanding of the major personality disorders includes an appreciation of some variations among the major personality disorders, particularly with regard to NPD. While Sharp's pivotal research supported the concept of a general factor common to serious personality pathology and recognized Kernberg's concept of borderline organization as the earliest formulation of this view, her research also found that three categorical personality disorder diagnoses remained distinct: narcissistic, schizotypal personality, and antisocial (Sharp et al., 2015). This supported Kernberg's longstanding formulation of NPD as centered around a particular psychological structure which he named the pathological grandiose self (PGS). Individuals with this self-representation appropriate all that is good (positive elements of the real self and idealized elements of the imagined self and others) and project all that is negative on the other and the outside world. The condensation of ideal and real elements of the self leads to a narrative that may stabilize the individual's sense of self, but that does not fully correspond to reality. The PGS emerges in individuals as a defensive structure. The basic stance of aggrandizing the self and devaluing all others defends against the narcissistic individual's core sense of vulnerability, emptiness, inferiority, and lack of value. The emptiness is rooted in attacks on the self that stem from punitive superego precursors that demand perfection of the self rather than developing into the psychic agency of an integrated superego that guides the individual without imposing the rigid demand of existing at the ideal level. This formulation corresponds to research findings that among patients with personality disorders, those with NPD are uniquely high on grandiosity, fantasies of unlimited success, sense of self as special and unique, and the need for excessive admiration (Gunderson and Ronningstam, 2001; Hilsenroth et al., 1998). However, recent research has affirmed Kernberg's original clinical observations that while grandiosity is a key distinguishing feature of narcissistic pathology, grandiosity and vulnerability exist in dynamic relation to each other in those with NPD (Diamond et al., 2022; Edershile et al., 2022).

Conclusion

In this chapter, we have presented Kernberg's model of structural diagnosis. This approach to diagnosis and classification of personality pathology has emerged from decades of clinical experience and is convergent with current empirical developments in the study of personality functioning and personality disorders. The ORT model of personality disorders provides clinicians with an important guide to understanding, evaluating, and classifying personality pathology and aids in adjusting the treatment to the type and level of pathology.

Note

1 It is important to appreciate the distinction between the DSM-5 borderline personality disorder (BPD) and the borderline level of personality organization (BPO). BPD is a specific personality disorder, diagnosed based on a constellation of descriptive features. BPO is a much broader category based on structural features. The BPO diagnosis subsumes the DSM-5 BPD as well as all of the syndromal personality disorders.

Chapter 4

Expanding the Boundaries of the Analytic Method and Focusing on the Central Techniques of Psychoanalysis as the Core of Psychoanalytic Training and Treatments

As mentioned in Chapter 1, Otto Kernberg's interest in personality disorders dates to early in his career. Treating patients with severe personality pathology in the long-term inpatient units of the Menninger Hospital, the New York State Psychiatric Institute, and the Westchester Division of the New York Presbyterian Hospital provided a special opportunity to study personality pathology and improve the treatment of personality disorders. Kernberg described (personal communication, January 14, 2023) his curiosity being aroused by an early experience at Menninger, trying to understand a patient who had been in the throes of an intense affect storm in a therapy session with him who he then observed speaking calmly with other patients immediately after leaving his office. Grounded in the psychoanalytic tradition, Kernberg strove to apply concepts and techniques from that model of treatment to patients who did not respond well to classical psychoanalysis.

Kernberg's writings in the 1970s, along with those of John Gunderson, helped establish borderline personality disorder (BPD) as a serious condition within the field of mental health, with BPD first being listed in the American Psychiatric Association's *Diagnostic and Statistical Manual* in 1980 (APA, 1980). Like Kernberg, Gunderson, who had established a center for BPD at Harvard's McLean Hospital, attracted a group of clinicians and scholars to advance his thinking and work. Though sharing roots in psychoanalysis, Gunderson's approach to BPD was more symptom-oriented in contrast to Kernberg's

DOI: 10.4324/9781003053415-4

focus on the underlying psychological structure. Gunderson developed a model of treatment, now known as "good psychiatric management" (Gunderson & Links, 2014), that focused on understanding the nature of BPD from the interpersonal perspective and helping the clinician provide the optimal combination of information, support, and questioning. Gunderson explicitly acknowledged distancing himself from his psychoanalytic roots (personal communication, November 8, 2017). Kernberg continued to focus on psychoanalytic principles and techniques, not out of stubborn loyalty but because of the conviction that a treatment that targets psychological structure and deep-seated intrapsychic conflict will provide the most profound and helpful change in the life of a patient with BPD. Even Gunderson, who took on the role of diplomat among the different models of treatment that had developed for BPD (dialectical behavioral therapy, schema therapy, mentalization-based therapy), acknowledged that transference-focused psychotherapy (TFP), which he believed to be the most complex treatment model, provided the most comprehensive level of help (Gunderson, Weill Cornell Medical College Psychiatry Grand Rounds, November 8, 2017).

As described in Chapter 3, Kernberg contributed an understanding of severe personality pathology that described borderline personality *organization* (BPO). BPO provided a broader conceptualization than the more symptom-based BPD that was inspired by Gunderson's descriptive conceptualization of the pathology. As we have pointed out, recent developments in both the DSM-5 Alternative Model for Personality Disorders and the International Classification of Diseases, Eleventh Revision (ICD-11) reflect an increasing acceptance of Kernberg's structural model of BPO as a way of describing personality disorders based on the individual's experience of self and others.

The core features of BPO are the predominance of splitting-based defense mechanisms, identity diffusion, pathology of object relations, and intact but fluctuating reality testing. Kernberg's description of the modifications of psychoanalytic techniques necessary to treat this patient population culminated in the development of TFP (Clarkin et al., 1999; Clarkin et al., 2006; Yeomans et al., 2015). In its original form, TFP is an empirically based, manualized psychodynamic psychotherapy that emerged from the psychoanalytic tradition as a long-term individual psychotherapy to meet the needs of patients with serious personality pathology. It has subsequently been adapted to extend to additional groups of patients and more diverse treatment conditions.

"Applied TFP" (Hersh et al., 2016) describes the use of TFP principles throughout the range of psychiatric/mental health settings. In addition to focusing on the importance of understanding any clinician-patient encounter in terms of the representations of self and other activated in the patient's mind, applied-TFP emphasizes openness to considering and sharing a diagnosis of personality disorder, early involvement of significant others in treatment, clear definition of roles and responsibilities for both the patient and the therapist, and continuous, dynamic attention to the therapeutic alliance that allows for adjustment and analysis as the relationship between the patient and the therapist evolves. "Extended TFP" (Caligor et al., 2018) adapts the model to treat all levels of personality difficulties, from BPO through neurotic personality organization and subsyndromal conditions characterized by problematic personality traits. "TFP-N" (Diamond et al., 2022) describes the TFP-object relations theory understanding of the narcissistic personality structure and modifications of the application of TFP techniques to effectively treat patients with narcissistic pathology. TFP has also been adapted to treat adolescents and children (Normandin et al., 2021).

In addition, as TFP became more clearly defined through the series of treatment manuals and empirical research, it has come to be considered a conceptual and technical model of therapy that can be used to introduce therapists in training to the principles of psychodynamic psychotherapy in a systematic way (Bernstein et al., 2015). Rather than narrating the evolution of TFP in detail, this chapter will provide the reader with a description of TFP in its current form and discuss its relation to other forms of psychoanalytic work.

The very idea of a "manual" for a psychoanalytically based psychotherapy seemed anathema to many trained in the psychoanalytic tradition. The main objection by psychoanalytic clinicians was that any attempt to systematize psychoanalysis or psychoanalytic psychotherapy would detract from the unique quality of each patient-therapist (analysand-analyst) pairing. Kernberg's justification for writing a manual was twofold. The first justification was his concern that the psychoanalytic literature, while offering an unequaled richness of thought about the mind and techniques of how to help resolve conflicts within the mind, did not provide a clear description of the systematic application of those techniques. The second justification, in line with Kernberg's emphasis on precise diagnosis, was that specific forms of pathology present in patterns that are recognizable and somewhat predictable and that it is possible to combine respect for the patient's individuality with awareness of the presentation of forms of pathology according to certain expectable patterns and that it helps the clinician to have an organized sense of how to respond to those patterns when they occur. In addition, the TFP "manuals" are not manuals in the strictest sense of the word. In contrast to cognitive behavioral therapy (CBT) manuals that may present a specific pattern of steps for the therapist to follow, and of homework or exercises for the patient to do, the TFP manuals are driven by principles that are described, leaving the precise application of the principles up to the discretion of the therapist. Development of the TFP manuals included the study of recorded therapy sessions. Kernberg and his colleagues at the Personality Disorders Institute (PDI) viewed videos of their work as a practical aide in distilling the essence of the work as it was applied with different individual styles by the members of the group.

As a model of psychodynamic psychotherapy, TFP retains the essential stance of exploration of unconscious motivations and conflicts as the core to achieving change in psychological structure with related improvements in the patient's subjective experience of self and others and in symptoms and behaviors. The basic mechanism of change is the transformation of enactments of conflicts involving split-off affect states into awareness and integration through the process of reflection on the patient's experiences of the therapist in the course of the therapy sessions. The most obvious differences from traditional analytic work have to do with the level of structure needed to work with patients with a borderline level of personality organization, which we will discuss in more detail after describing the assessment phase of TFP.

In keeping with Kernberg's interest in the importance of accurate diagnosis for guiding treatment, he developed the "structural interview" described in Chapter 5. The challenge of reliably carrying out this interview led to the development of a number of more structured assessment instruments: the Inventory of Personality Organization (IPO; Lenzenweger et al., 2001), a self-report measure, the Structured Interview for Personality Organization (STIPO; Clarkin et al., 2004; Clarkin et al., 2017), a clinical interview, the STIPO-R for Adolescents (Weiner et al., 2023), and the Levels of Personality Organization and Development questionnaire (LPODq) (Biberdzic et al., 2023).

In TFP, an important distinction is made between the first meetings with the patient that are preparation for therapy and the therapy itself. The principle underlying this position is that therapy cannot take place until an agreement has been reached between the patient and the therapist about the nature of the patient's difficulties and an appropriate treatment frame has been established. The diagnostic sessions establish the nature of the patient's condition, whether it falls in the range of personality pathology and, if so, what level and type of personality pathology.

The information derived from the assessment sessions guides the therapist in their specific treatment recommendation and in the specifics of the treatment contract and frame (Yeomans et al., 1992). Before beginning the discussion of the treatment contract, the therapist describes their diagnostic impression to the patient in simple, "user-friendly", language. The therapist communicates their view that the patient's difficulties are centered around problems in the patient's sense of self and experience of others and that such difficulties are at the core of what we call "personality disorders". The therapist, after establishing whether the patient is willing to consider this way of seeing their problems and in keeping with the principle of informed consent, goes on to describe the different treatments that can be considered and why they are recommending a psychoanalytic, exploratory form of therapy (if that is the case). The therapist then, as part of establishing the treatment frame, gives a simple description of psychoanalytic therapy, explaining that the root of the patient's emotional and behavioral difficulties is believed to be in conflicting emotional states within the patient's mind and that the therapy will seek to help the patient become aware of elements in their mind of which they are not aware that have an impact on how they feel, think, and behave. The description of the model of treatment also makes clear that the therapist's role is not to provide direct support or opinions since doing so would detract from the goal of increasing the patient's autonomy.

If the patient agrees to, or at least is willing to consider, the diagnosis of personality disorder, the therapist moves on to discussing the conditions that need to be in place to engage in the treatment. The structure, or frame, of the treatment serves multiple functions in TFP. First, it limits acting out behaviors to encourage the experiencing and containment of affects that the patient traditionally discharged through action. Second, it provides a scaffolding for the complicated therapeutic alliance that develops with BPO patients. By virtue of the patient's split internal world, a therapy that includes technical neutrality (to be more fully described below) will necessarily include moments of intense negative/paranoid transference. Such transferences are necessary to bring about the eventual goal of psychological integration, but they present a challenge to the development of the therapeutic alliance. It is for this reason that more supportive therapies that emphasize the need for an explicit positive therapeutic alliance from the beginning of therapy have difficulty integrating the patient's split internal world since the negative transference tends to be deflected onto objects outside the therapeutic setting. In TFP, the carefully elaborated treatment frame helps maintain a commitment to the therapy by both parties when emotional intensity emerges in the sessions. The third reason for the importance of the treatment structure/frame is its role in the interpretive process. As therapy proceeds, both the patient and the therapist are subject to internal pressures to deviate from the exploratory treatment frame when emotionally charged internal object relations dyads are activated in the session. For example, the therapist may experience the urge to extend the time of the session and feel that they would be a callous, uncaring person if they ended the session on time. Recalling the treatment frame (the agreement to meet for 45-minute sessions) helps the therapist distinguish between external reality ("I am doing what we agreed to".) and the patient's projection onto the therapist of an image from their internal world ("I am a neglectful and depriving person if I end the session on time".). Deviating from the frame (extending the time of the session in this case) might de-escalate the anxiety that arises when a split-off part of the patient's internal world (in this case, the experience of the other as neglectful and uncaring, and the related feelings of anger and hatred) is activated. However, the work of integration of the split internal world is not possible without the emergence of this material in the lived experience within the session. Hence, the therapist takes note of any temptation to deviate from the frame and of any actual deviations on their part or on the patient's part and encourages reflection on them as possible attempts to avoid the emergence of intense internal affect states (Delaney and Yeomans, 2021).

The contracting phase of setting up the therapy can be roughly divided into two parts. The first part describes the respective roles of the patient and the therapist in any exploratory psychodynamic psychotherapy. The role of the patient is to attend regularly, to report as freely as possible all that passes through their mind with some eventual connection to the problems that brought them to treatment, and to take responsibility for payment. The role of the therapist is to provide regular sessions in which all feelings are welcome and to try to help the patient become aware of unknown parts of the self. While delineating these roles may seem very basic, it is essential to do so with patients whose pathology leads them to often act in different ways than what was described as their role and/or expect the therapist to behave in ways that diverge from the therapist's described role. The patient's divergences from the agreed-upon roles provide material for the work of transference analysis described below: understanding and interpreting elements of the patient's internal world as they unfold in the patient's experience of the therapist.

The second part of the contracting process involves establishing parameters around any form of acting out that has been part of the patient's history. Acting out, in addition to being a resistance to internal experience, may also put the patient's, or others', well-being at risk. The therapist empathizes with the patient's struggles with self-control but encourages the patient to find a measure of control within themselves that, by virtue of their misunderstanding of personality disorders ("people with personality disorders have absolutely no ability to control themselves"), they may not have tried to exert before. This part of the contracting can have a behavioral quality as the therapist and the patient discuss what the patient's responsibilities will be in relation to whatever form(s) of acting out have characterized their history. Forms of acting out could include suicide attempts, other self-destructive behaviors, aggression towards others, substance abuse, eating disorders, noncompliance with medical treatments, dishonest communication, inconsistent participation in therapy, intrusions into the therapist's life, a passive lifestyle with no consistent involvement in a regular activity, or any number of other possible behaviors.

The framing of the treatment also includes a discussion of clear goals of therapy beyond containing acting out, which is a preliminary step towards more ambitious goals. TFP encourages establishing specific goals in place of the vague "I want to understand myself better". The TFP therapist's position is that it does not make sense to engage in a therapy that requires intensive work on the part of both the patient and the therapist if the two do not agree on major life goals, such as being able to maintain a stable intimate relationship or invest consistently in studies or work. These goals are in addition to the desired improvement in symptoms, such as affect lability or self-harming behaviors, and have to do with the change in psychological structure – the integration of radically polarized internal affect states and the consequent shift in subjective sense of self and others – that is at the core of the treatment. It is important to note that the therapist's attitude in the process of setting up the treatment is not neutral; the therapist will agree to therapy only if there is a consensus about positive life goals. The therapist's attitude throughout the contracting process is to describe the treatment that they recommend while not imposing it. The choice of treatment is in the hands of the patient. The therapist is not neutral in their description of what they recommend. It is if the patient has agreed to the treatment that the therapist assumes a position of technical neutrality, as described below.

The extent of the preparation for beginning the treatment described above differs from what is done in most psychoanalytic psychotherapy. An additional distinguishing element is the possible inclusion of a family meeting in setting up the treatment. In cases where the patient, of whatever age, is highly dependent on parents or partner, a meeting with those persons and the patient can be important to (1) clarify the others' understanding of the problem and (2) explore any secondary gain of illness the family might be providing and discuss how best to limit that. Parents or partner who believe the patient is suffering from depression or anxiety and who have no concept of personality disorder are likely, with the best of intentions, to provide unhealthy secondary gains.

If the therapist and the patient come to an agreement about the conditions of treatment, the therapy begins. At that point, the patient is invited to assume their role of reporting the thoughts and feelings that come to mind. As mentioned above, Kernberg was concerned about the psychoanalytic literature's lack of a systematic exposition of how to guide the analyst/therapist in the application of analytic techniques. A goal of the TFP manuals was to fill that gap. The manuals encourage the therapist to think of the work of therapy on three broad levels: the strategies, the tactics, and the techniques of treatment. This conceptualization of the work is to help the therapist organize their understanding of all the myriad material to which they are exposed in therapy sessions.

Strategies of treatment. The strategies of TFP encourage the therapist to always keep in mind the overarching goal of therapy with BPO patients when listening to the different channels of communication in the session: to achieve integration of a split and fragmented internal world. This overall strategy is in keeping with the Kleinian concepts of the paranoid-schizoid position and the depressive position. The internal split at the core of BPO is based on the patient's projection of unacknowledged aggressive affects onto others so that approaching others is fraught with anxiety related to paranoid fears. As maladaptive as this splitting may be, it protects the individual from the painful awarenesses that accompany the psychological integration of the depressive position: first, awareness of one's own aggression and the damage it can cause and, second, awareness that the image of the perfect provider that existed in the positive, ideal segment of the split internal world does not exist in reality. The overarching trajectory of TFP is to help people shift from the paranoid-schizoid psychological organization to the more complex and reality-based depressive organization. The path is difficult because of the pain in seeing beyond the primitive splitting defenses. Nevertheless, the goal can be achieved, albeit with the understanding that, under stressful circumstances, any individual who functions primarily in terms of the depressive position can regress to the comforting but dangerous simplicity of the paranoid-schizoid position. This will be discussed further in relation to group functioning in Chapter 7.

To assist the therapist in maintaining adherence to the ultimate goal of integration, TFP encourages the therapist to keep the following strategies in mind: (1) to discern the object relations dyad that is active in the moment in the session and to help the patient become aware of it, (2) to bring the patient's attention to role reversals when they occur within the dyad that is being experienced (this is the single most difficult step of TFP since it involves the patient considering that what they are projecting may exist within themselves), and (3) to help the patient become aware of the radically polarized experiences that they have at different times in relation to the therapist and to help them understand the motivations for this separation of extreme affect states. It is important to note that the dyad, or patient's experience of the therapist in a given moment, may, at times, be explicitly stated by the patient (e.g., "You looked at the clock so I can see you want to get rid of me".) or, more subtly, may be implicit as in the case of a patient who incessantly repeats problems and complaints to the therapist without any apparent reflection on them. In this latter case, the dyad may be the patient experiencing him or her self as a helpless individual appealing for a cure from an imagined omnipotent caretaker.

Tactics of treatment. The second level of attention for the therapist to keep in mind is that of the therapy tactics. The tactics are those elements of the treatment that need to be in place to effectively employ the treatment techniques, described below. Working with BPO patients requires special attention to this level of the therapy because BPO patients' splitting defenses and tendency to act out intolerable affect states render therapies with inadequate attention to the conditions of treatment likely to become chaotic. The strengthening of the structure of the treatment, initially through the contracting process described above, was the first distinct change from more traditional psychoanalytic work as Kernberg developed the treatment modifications needed to treat patients with BPO.

After the establishment of the treatment frame, the most important tactics as the therapy proceeds are maintaining the frame and choosing the most important material around which to intervene. As treatment moves forward, the work of tactfully shedding light on the patient's defenses, embodied in activated object relations dyads, inevitably provokes anxiety in the session. Attempting to escape from the anxiety, patients are at risk of acting out (e.g., self-harm or substance abuse), of defensively using the associative process (e.g., trivialization and splitting off of segments of their internal world or external life), or of acting in their external life in ways that undermine the work of the therapy (e.g., absenteeism at work or dropping out of college). Therapists, who are also susceptible to the discomfort of anxiety in sessions, are at risk of shifting from exploratory work to more overtly supportive work. Ongoing awareness of the frame, and attention to any deviation from it on the part of the patient or the therapist, alert the therapist to these defensive enactments and the need to reflect upon and interpret them.

The choice of what material to address is an ongoing challenge in sessions as the therapist attends to the verbal, nonverbal, and countertransference channels of communication. The challenge is compounded with BPO patients since there can be abrupt shifts in the patient's associations and can be discrepancies among the different channels of communication. TFP guides the therapist in their choice of material by emphasizing the need to (1) pursue what is most affectively charged; (2) follow a system that prioritizes material according to any risk to safety to self or others, or any threat to the continuation of therapy that may be present; and (3) respect the analytic principle of generally proceeding from surface to depth, from defense to impulse except in emergency situations that might call for early deep interpretation.

Treatment techniques. Adhering to the tactics of treatment serves the purpose of allowing the effective implementation of the therapeutic techniques. Discussion of techniques gets to the heart of Kernberg's thinking about psychoanalysis and psychoanalytic therapy. He proposes that four basic techniques underlie all psychoanalytically inspired work and that the difference between psychoanalysis, exploratory psychoanalytic therapy, and supportive psychoanalytic therapy lies in the emphasis that is, or is not, put on each of techniques in the various types of therapeutic endeavor.

The techniques are:

1   maintenance and use of technical neutrality
2   awareness and use of countertransference
3   the interpretive process, and
4   transference analysis as the subset of the broader interpretive process that is most relevant to psychological change in patients with severe personality disorders.

Technical neutrality. This is an attitude of concerned objectivity on the part of the therapist that avoids siding with any of the elements of the patient's intrapsychic conflict but, rather, maintains an observing distance from those elements of conflicts and attempts to engage the patient in a reflection on them in contrast to acting out or projecting a part of a conflict. Neutrality does not mean having a detached, indifferent attitude towards the patient, but it does involve an attitude that must be learned since it can feel counter to the natural human response to react supportively to explicit or implicit appeals for reassurance or validation from the patient or to respond defensively or with counterattacks to criticisms from the patient. The goal of neutrality is to avoid supporting one side or another of a patient's internal conflict in a way that would relieve the patient of the internal experience of the conflict and to help the patient reflect on the conflicting forces present within them. An example is to refrain, when asked, from giving an opinion as to whether a patient was right or wrong to not call their mother on Mother's Day, but rather to help the patient better understand the libidinal affects (e.g., affection, longing for closeness) and aggressive affects (e.g., frustration, envy, hatred) present in them in relation to their mother and, especially in the early phases of therapy, in relation to internal representations of mother that may overshadow a more accurate but complex objective view of their mother.

Maintaining technical neutrality often provokes transference reactions ("You are depriving me of what I need from you by not telling what you think!"), which can lead to the next level of exploration, reflecting on the feeling that the therapist is callous and depriving and what might motivate that. A commitment to maintaining neutrality also helps the therapist be alert to countertransference reactions. A therapist might feel: "Maybe I am being mean by not telling the patient my opinion since it may relieve her anxiety (in the moment) for me to say what I think". Such reflections on the part of the therapist are related to the challenge of distinguishing what part of the experience in the session corresponds to the patient's internal world and what part is related to objective reality. The therapist faced with this question is helped by comparing what is going on in the session to the frame of the treatment and can orient themselves in relation to the frame. In this instance, the therapist would remind themselves that they proposed an exploratory therapy to the patient and the patient accepted. Their initial description of the therapy included making it clear that the therapist's role in exploratory therapy is not to give opinions or advice but rather to help the patient understand their internal conflicts. With this mental check, the therapist can be reassured that not answering the question is not an act of meanness but that that idea is related to a projection that should be explored.

To summarize, maintaining neutrality redirects conflicts back to their place of origin in the patient's mind. In so doing, neutrality implicitly confronts projective defenses and therefore can provoke anxiety in sessions, which is the principal reason that therapists have difficulty adhering to this fundamental technique of treatment.

Deviations from neutrality. In keeping with the need to modify the basic techniques according to the patient's level of pathology and the nature and goals of the treatment, TFP for BPO patients includes the understanding that the therapist may at times have to deviate from a position of neutrality and that the knowledge of when and how to do this is part of the proper application of TFP. This understanding stems from the fact that BPO patients may act in ways that are dangerous to themselves, to others, and/or to the treatment. If such a situation arises and cannot be successfully worked on by the interpretive process, the therapist's role is to deviate from neutrality – to take a clear position in relation to an issue – and then, when the situation has been resolved, to explore and interpret the interaction the patient has provoked. An example is that of a young adult patient with a history of suicide attempts whose initial transference was to experience her therapist as a "cold robot" because of the treatment frame that limited communication between sessions. Two months into treatment, the patient casually mentioned that her new boyfriend had brought up the idea that they consider a murder-suicide pact. The therapist explored this with the patient and suggested it might be the patient's way of expressing anger at the therapist for his perceived coldness and a way of provoking the therapist to become more actively involved with her. The patient seemed indifferent to the interpretation and stated provocatively that she "just liked" the new boyfriend and that the therapist should not worry. At that point, the therapist deviated from neutrality and expressed the firm position that the patient should end the relation. The patient did end the relationship, and, after she had done so, the therapist could return to the interpretive process and propose that the patient lived with the assumption that no one cared about her until evidence proved otherwise and that she had the choice of either continuing her pattern of entering into dangerous situations to provoke temporary evidence that another person cared about her, as she had provoked him to provide by his deviation from neutrality, or exploring her basic assumption regarding uncaring others, with the possibility of modifying that assumption and moving beyond it.

Countertransference. Kernberg emphasizes the need to consider countertransference in the broad sense: both the therapist's transference to the patient and the therapist's reactions to the patient's transference(s). It is this latter part that is particularly important in the work with BPO patients where complementary countertransference and projective identification play an important role in accessing split-off aspects of the patient's internal world that the patient manages to deny in themselves and activate in others. Nevertheless, it is the responsibility of the therapist to continually monitor which elements of the countertransference originate in their own issues and which elements originate in the patient. Kernberg also emphasizes the need to be attentive to the chronic countertransference developments that are generally more subtle and more difficult to perceive than acute countertransferences.

In TFP, the therapist reflects on their countertransference to better understand split-off parts of the patient's internal world. The therapist does not directly state how they feel, or are made to feel, but rather understands the feeling as representing an internal object that the patient cannot tolerate. Rather than direct disclosure of countertransference, the therapist refers to a feeling "in the room". For example, "It's as though something hateful is involved here", or "There might be an erotic feeling to think about". In this way, countertransference is used as an important element in the construction of the transference interpretation, starting with the first TFP strategy of understanding the dyad that is active in the moment. In situations where countertransference dominates, the discussion of the dyad can start with naming the affect that links the self and object representations in the dyad and then move on to sorting out the relation of self and object to the affect.

The interpretive process. Kernberg emphasizes that interpretation unfolds as a process in contrast to the outdated and generally discredited simplistic view that it is an explanation that the therapist provides the patient. Kernberg describes three steps in the interpretive process: clarification, confrontation, and interpretation itself.

With patients suffering from severe personality disorders, the initial work that may be required before more traditional interpretation can be used effectively involves helping patients contain intense affects that they experience without yet cognitively containing the affects in words. In this early phase of therapy, there is an emphasis on describing the object relations dyad the patient is experiencing, simply putting it into words, without questioning it. Such work has been referred to as using therapist-centered interpretations (Steiner, 1994) or interpreting within the projection. It helps the patient gain a fuller awareness of states that exist within them that are, as yet, intolerable to experience as part of the self but may be reflected upon as part of the interaction that is connected with the object. The therapist's ability to describe the patient's experience of the interaction can be experienced as empathic, even if the experience being described is negative.

Clarification refers to asking the patient for more information about something they have brought up. This is another way in which TFP deviates from a model of pure free association. Clarification may appear to be an anodyne process, but it can challenge the defensive system of BPO patients since their internal narrative is often characterized by gaps or inconsistencies that correspond to the split fragmentation of their inner world. Asking for clarification of a point may lead to an uneasy preconscious awareness of an inconsistency that protects from an awareness, so the therapist must proceed with empathy and tact.

The predominance of splitting defenses in BPO patients leads to the gaps, inconsistencies, and possible contradictions in their material. The interpretive step of confrontation consists of the therapist's expression of interest in and curiosity about these gaps or contradictions. While the term "confrontation" may have a hostile connotation, the therapeutic technique is closer to the etymology of the word: putting two things face-to-face. Therapeutic confrontation involves communications from the patient (that could include nonverbal communication) that do not seem to "add up" and may represent split-off parts of the patient's psyche. The therapist puts them face-to-face to encourage reflection on the defensive internal fragmentation and the mental states represented by the different contradictory parts of the patient's communications (Kivity et al., 2021).

As the stepwise interpretive process moves forward, the patient's response to a therapist's confrontation might activate a reflective response in the patient that leads to the understanding that would have been the therapist's interpretation. In such instances, the therapist does not have to advance to the interpretation itself since the patient has done so (e.g., the patient who says "I guess I tend to miss sessions after we've had a session with a good, positive feeling because there's something about being close to you that freaks me out…. I guess that's the next thing to think about".).

Interpretations per se are hypotheses about the motivations for maintaining the splitting-based defenses. They often are related to understanding the protections against anxiety that the primitive defenses at the root of the paranoid-schizoid organization offer. For example:

> The tendency to withdraw after you feel any closeness here may have to do with fear that the experience of closeness might include some moments of disappointment, and that could lead to a devastating feeling of having lost a kind of perfect caring that you hoped you had found here.
>
> (interpreting the fear of having to give up the internal ideal object)

Transference analysis. This subset of the broader interpretive process gives TFP its name. It is the form of interpretation that focuses on the here-and-now experience of the relationship with the therapist and the distortions of that relationship that result from the projection of internal object representations. Since the focus is on distortions of the therapeutic relationship that can be used as windows into the patient's internal world, it is essential that the therapy begin with a clear description of the respective roles of the patient and the therapist at the beginning of the therapy, as described above, to establish the nature of the real therapeutic relation. Brief examples of entering into the process of transference analysis were seen above in the discussion of the treatment frame ("Am I a cold therapist if I end the session on time?") and of neutrality ("Am I cruel and depriving if I do not give that patient my opinion?").

While the concept of transference analysis is clear, supervision, over many years, has revealed therapists' general tendency to favor discussion of the verbal content of the patient's communication over the exploration of the implicit interaction. It is often difficult for the therapist to maintain the dual roles of offering themselves as the transferential object and maintaining an observing stance in relation to the activated transference. It is important to avoid prematurely referring the projection back to the patient's internal world. In the example of not answering the patient's direct question about not calling on Mother's Day, the comment "So you *see me* as cruel and depriving you of what you need", implicitly tells the patient that what they feel is wrong and even blames the patient for their inaccurate perception. A more neutral intervention that is in line with promoting reflection is "So I could be a person who is cruel and depriving you of what you need". While it is a subtle difference, the second intervention leaves the patient's internal representation hovering between them to be reflected upon. In addition, the therapist's ability to entertain the possibility that they could be a cruel and depriving object is an implicit suggestion that this might not be the case since the therapist is willing to consider it.

As splitting defenses are interpreted, the patient's internal world becomes more complex. The superficial and rigid representations of self and others begin to shift to richer and nuanced representations. Those primitive defenses begin to give way to more evenly functioning repression-based defenses. Internal conflicts become less intense and extreme as they become more complex. This complexity includes the emergence of more triadic, Oedipally related conflicts in contrast to dyadic relational structures, although the work with BPO patients may present with some rudimentary Oedipal issues from the early stages of treatment (Diamond & Yeomans, 2007).

Narcissistic personality disorder (NPD) as a variant of BPO. The pathological grandiose self (PGS) was described briefly at the end of Chapter 3 as a psychological structure that absorbs all that is positive into the self and projects all that is negative onto others. It is a defensive narrative of the self that protects the individual from an underlying core sense of fragmentation, emptiness, hopelessness, and frustration, but that can be subject to moments of vulnerable collapse.

The PGS has an impact on the NPD patient's presentation and response to treatment. While BPD patients most frequently present with a predominant dyad of victim in relation to persecutor with frequent role reversals within that dyad (the patient shifting back and forth between the victim role and the aggressor role), the core dyad in NPD patients is typically of the superior self in relation to the devalued other.

That dyad tends to stubbornly predominate in NPD patients in a way that does not provide the therapist with the frequent windows into internal fragmentation that are present in work with classic borderline patients with their regular role reversals and abrupt shifts from one dyad to another. Related to this is the finding that NPD patients are more likely to present with a dismissing internal model of attachment in contrast to the preoccupied unresolved attachment that is more common in BPD patients. Since the focus of a dismissing attachment style is continuously away from attachment relationships, NPD patients generally do not initially display the intense transferences typical of BPD patients.

These characteristics of NPD patients present particular treatment challenges that are discussed in the book describing TFP for NPD (Diamond et al., 2022). The essence of the therapeutic work involves analyzing the grandiose/idealized and vulnerable/devalued aspects of PGS in order to gain access to the fragmented world of intense and distressing internal object relations against which the PGS defends. The therapy can then focus on the internal states and anxieties that are at the core of NPD as they are of other BPO pathology. Therapy with NPD patients must be carried out with a particular tact that involves the therapist containing and working within the projection of aspects of the self that the patient cannot accept for longer periods than is typically the case with BPD patients. This tact and patience is required because of the emergence of intense depressive affects as the therapy leads to awareness in the patient of both those unwanted aspects of the self, such as aggressive feelings or dependency longings, and of the costs and consequences that resulted from the grandiose system that defended against them. Feelings of guilt and remorse for the damage caused by the narcissistic defenses and remorse over lost opportunities for meaningful investments in life hearken the development of the depressive position. TFP with NPD patients advances by working through the narcissistic defenses to gain access to the identity fragmentation and conflicts around dependency fears and wishes, and between aggressive and libidinal affects, that are at the core of all patients with BPO.

The evolution of the therapy. If the TFP process moves forward in the optimal way, the BPO patient's psychological structure and conflicts shift to the neurotic level. As part of this process of psychological integration, the patient's internal world becomes structured in a way that is closer to Freud's tripartite model. Progress towards integration is not linear. Early experiences of integration cause anxiety. Awareness that previously projected aggressive affects (e.g., anger, destructiveness, hatred) may exist in the self is an unfamiliar experience that involves guilt but also involves the fragile emergence of moments of trust. The anxiety of these unfamiliar states generally provokes periods of regression to the more familiar, if less positive and adaptive, paranoid position.

As the patient's psychological structure becomes more integrated, with a more consolidated sense of self and others and the predominance of repression-based defenses, the therapeutic work shifts to the kind of psychodynamic exploratory therapy that analytically trained therapists are generally more familiar with. Work at this level of psychological organization can be done within the TFP-object relations model that is referred to as "extended TFP" and is described in *Psychodynamic Therapy for Personality Pathology: Treating Self and Interpersonal Functioning* (Caligor et al., 2018). Extended TFP broadens the application of TFP principles and techniques to the full range of personality pathology, including the neurotic range and subsyndromal problematic personality traits. Extended TFP can be used with patients who initially present with pathology at a higher level than the borderline range as well as with patients with typical BPO pathology as it follows them from the initial split and fragmented psychological structure to a more integrated organization.

Looking forward to the range of psychoanalytic work. As Kernberg's reflection on the range of psychoanalytically based clinical interventions has advanced, he proposes organizing our conceptualization of the different types of psychoanalytic treatments according to the manner in which the four basic techniques are applied. This way of thinking reflects the fact that, while TFP was developed as an extension of the psychoanalytic method for a specific patient population, the practice of TFP has helped to develop a more nuanced understanding of these techniques and how to apply them in response to different forms of psychopathology, leading Kernberg to recently write about the mutual influences of psychoanalysis and TFP (Kernberg, 2021).

The analytic setting of three or four sessions per week with patients on the couch who, for the most part, can participate in the process of free association corresponds to Loewald's (1960) description of the psychoanalytic situation: the encounter between a patient who comes to treatment seeking help and willing to explore their inner experience with the trusting expectation that the analyst has an honest interest in helping him without being omniscient. In this situation, the analyst can generally prioritize the verbal channel of communication over the nonverbal. However, the impact of intense caricatured internal representations of self and others, rooted in splitting defenses, leads BPO patients to dramatic regressions in the classical analytic setting. Depending on the level of pathology and the circumstances and goals of treatment, when working with these patients, the therapist must consider how best to apply the techniques of neutrality, countertransference, interpretation, and transference analysis in an overall frame that generally involves twice-weekly face-to-face sessions.

Neutrality. Psychoanalysis is characterized by the most consistent maintenance of neutrality in sessions in comparison to TFP and supportive psychodynamic therapy, with less need to emphasize establishing and maintaining the frame of treatment than in those forms of therapy. TFP calls for generally maintaining neutrality, with appropriate deviations as described above, while supportive therapy has less of a stress on maintaining neutrality. An additional aspect of TFP that may appear to move away from a position of neutrality is the therapist's periodic need to represent reality in working with patients whose internal representations may compromise their judgment. An example is that of a patient with NPD whose grandiose self-representation keeps him from seeing that repeated absenteeism puts his job at risk. After seeking clarification of the extent of the patient's thoughts about this, a therapist statement that "Most workplaces don't tolerate absenteeism indefinitely" would not be considered a deviation from neutrality. Simply put: to represent reality is not an abandonment of neutrality. The therapy process would then go on to explore what might be behind the patient's denial of this aspect of reality.

Countertransference. In TFP, the containing function of countertransference is emphasized more than in psychoanalysis because of the intense affective charge of split-off parts of the self that are activated by projective identification. BPO patients' tendency to deny elements of external reality may create intense countertransference anxiety. In response to this, the therapist may make reference to the element of external reality, as mentioned above. Working with BPO patients requires the therapist to tolerate primitive fantasies involving aggression, intense desire, envy, sadomasochistic issues, and other strong affects. It also requires the therapist to, with one part of the self, take on the role that the patient needs to cast them into while still maintaining neutrality and observing (the third position). Also, BPO patients are more likely to alternately activate concordant and complementary countertransference reactions in the therapist, allowing the therapist to identify with both the patient's conscious experience in the moment and their unintegrated internal objects. The therapist's ability to tolerate these fluctuating identifications and affects allows for understanding and interpretation of the corresponding fantasies, ultimately offering the patient a cognitive frame for previously inchoate affect states.

The interpretative process. Both psychoanalysis and TFP rely on the interpretive process to help the patient gain awareness of urges, thoughts, and affects against which they are defending. The nature of the defenses in higher-level and lower-level patients has an impact on the application of the interpretive process. The splitting-based defenses that predominate in lower-level patients call for containment and identification of split-off affect states that may not be necessary in higher-level patients. Splitting defenses also necessitate more attention to the nonverbal and countertransference channels of communication than is the case with higher-level patients in analysis or analytic therapy. Work with lower-level patients generally requires more emphasis on the initial clarification stage of the interpretive process than with higher-level patients because of frequent concrete quality of the affective states involved in lower-level patients' transferences.

Interpretation in any form of analytic work generally proceeds from surface to depth, addressing the defense before the impulse being defended against. This general rule comes with two caveats in working with BPO patients since these patients present with conflicts in which the material is affectively dissociated, in contrast to neurotic patients who present with unknown repressed material. First, unlike the repression-based defenses characteristic of neurotic patients that present as a stable and consistent defensive system, splitting-based defenses are such that what is defense and what is defended against can exchange places. Paranoid and aggressive feelings may defend against libidinal urges and longings at one moment, and then, at another moment, their positions can flip so that the libidinal urges defend against the aggression-laden affects. For this reason, work with lower-level patients challenges the concept of approaching analytic material with neither memory nor desire. Patients with major ego weakness may need certain ego functions of the therapist – memory of the earlier state in this case – to enter into the reflective process needed to address the conflict. This is especially important when the power of the patient's internal representations creates a merging in their mind of the activated dyad and external reality.

The second caveat with regard to working from surface to depth is related to the fact that BPO patients can be at risk of acting out in dangerous ways that include self-harm, harm to others, and abandoning the therapy. If such a risk is present, along with the possibility of temporarily deviating from neutrality discussed above, the therapist may shift immediately to the deepest level of interpretation in an attempt to avoid the acting out.

Transference analysis. This technique is central to psychoanalysis and TFP but less so to supportive psychodynamic psychotherapy. In TFP, analysis of the transference emphasizes the complete dyadic unit, emphasizing both the self-experience and the experience of the therapist as object. Psychoanalysis may not require as much emphasis on the self-representation since the neurotic patient has a more integrated sense of self than BPO patients and therefore a generally more consistent experience of self. BPO patients may overtly or subtly enact a variety of self-representations that complement the projected object representation. In addition, the BPO patient is likely to exhibit role reversals within a specific dyad that are not characteristic of neurotic patients. The interpretive process with BPO patients should include the place of each participant in the dyad with awareness of the likelihood of role reversals.

Transference work with BPO patients that takes place in the context of technical neutrality creates the possibility of periods of transference psychosis in which reality testing is temporarily lost and the patient is not capable of any observing distance with regard to the activated dyad and the present relationship with the therapist. Careful and tactful use of clarification and confrontation can generally engage the patient's reflective capacities, although the therapist may sometimes have to employ the technique of "incompatible realities" (Kernberg, 2021).

The primacy of transference analysis in working with BPO patients includes deferring some more classical parts of psychoanalytic work to later in the therapy. Dream analysis is an example. In working with low-level patients, the therapist defers detailed analysis of the content of and associations to the dream in favor of the more basic question of "What dyad is active in this patient's bringing up this material with me now?" In other words, the therapist respects the first TFP strategy: describing the active object relations dyad. In this case, is the patient looking for a magical explanation of the dream from the therapist, or might they be trying to please the therapist by offering a dream, or might they be challenging the therapist to see which of them can have the better dream interpretation? With lower-level patients, it is essential to get to know the various personae – the representations of self and other – who populate the patient's internal work and to achieve some integration of this internal world, before it is possible to enter into the full richness of the analytic process.

In summarizing Kernberg's current thinking about psychoanalytic education, he places the learning of the four basic techniques at the center of training. After these techniques are fully understood, he proposes establishing clarity about how they are differentially applied in psychoanalysis, exploratory psychoanalytic psychotherapy as embodied by TFP, and supportive psychoanalytic psychotherapy. This position reflects the impact of developing TFP on Kernberg's thinking about psychoanalysis. While TFP was developed to extend the range of the application of psychoanalysis, the experience of working with TFP has, in turn, helped better understand ways to use the basic analytic techniques in all forms of their application.

Chapter 5

Encouragement and Development of Research

One of the most important ways in which Otto Kernberg has been a pioneer in advancing psychoanalysis is his emphasis on the role of research. Beginning with his participation in the Menninger Psychotherapy Research Project, mentioned in Chapter 1 (Wallerstein et al., 1956), Kernberg dedicated a significant amount of his academic activity to research in diagnosis, psychopathology, psychotherapy, and, to some degree, neurobiology.

The Menninger Project, of which Kernberg was a charter member, was the most important early research on psychoanalysis and psychoanalytic psychotherapy. Psychoanalytic psychotherapy had been developing in clinics and hospitals beginning in the 1940s. As in other psychiatric hospitals, clinicians at Menninger used psychoanalytic techniques within the controlled and relatively safe hospital environment. These circumstances allowed for regression in the transference. This type of regression was beneficial for many patients but, in the case of patients with fragile ego strength and fragile reality testing, most of whom suffered from borderline personality disorder (BPD), could lead to regressive states that were not amenable to the therapeutic interventions used at that time. This situation required modifications in technique. Some of the modifications were generally accepted, such as having the patient sit up versus remaining on the analytic couch and decreasing the frequency of sessions. Beyond those changes, there were differences in the direction that analytic therapies took – differences that continue to this day and have a major impact on how psychodynamic psychotherapy is practiced. Some clinicians modified their work by including more cognitive-behavioral interventions, giving direct support in the form of advice giving, problem-solving, and avoiding transference exploration. Others, including Kernberg, emphasized (1) the need

DOI: 10.4324/9781003053415-5

for the therapist to generally maintain a stance of technical neutrality while allowing moments of strategic deviation from it, (2) a long phase of focusing on the techniques of clarification and confrontation before employing interpretations, and (3) increasing the early use of the countertransference and transference exploration. These latter elements were consistent with Kleinian views in contrast to an ego psychology perspective, and they form the core of what was to become transference-focused psychotherapy (TFP). As TFP developed, it also became clear that work with borderline patients also required more emphasis on the treatment frame and on limit-setting than was included in traditional psychoanalysis and most supportive psychodynamic psychotherapy.

The Menninger study included 42 patients, 21 of whom were treated with psychoanalysis and 21 with psychoanalytic psychotherapy. This research was carried out during a period of hubris in the psychoanalytic world. Psychoanalysis was considered by some to be an effective model of treatment across a large spectrum of psychiatric conditions. That overreach contributed to the subsequent devaluing of psychoanalysis in many quarters of psychiatry (Lieberman & Ogas, 2015). Since the 1980s, the pendulum has swung in the opposite direction, with biological psychiatry becoming guilty of hubris. Kernberg's position has been consistently integrative: while dedicated to psychoanalysis, he regularly studies developments in the neurosciences that advance our understanding of personality and personality disorders.

In the context of the emphasis on psychoanalysis prevalent in the 1960s, the results of the Menninger Project were surprising to some of its authors. The overall finding was that the severely ill patients in the study did better in psychoanalytic psychotherapy than in pure psychoanalysis. This led Robert Wallerstein, the head of the study, to promote the more directly supportive elements found in psychoanalytic psychotherapy described above (advice giving, avoiding transference interpretations, etc.). Kernberg, however, chose to study the cases in the psychotherapy cell of the Menninger study with particular attention to the nature of those therapies. In looking at the specific cases, he observed that the most severely ill patients did best in those psychotherapies in which the therapist emphasized a level of neutrality and transference analysis over overtly supportive interventions. This interest in the distinction between exploratory psychoanalytic psychotherapy in contrast to supportive psychoanalytic therapy has continued to be a focus of Kernberg's work throughout his career and may be the feature that most clearly distinguishes TFP from the more broadly

applied and less clearly defined supportive psychoanalytic psychotherapy. It is important to note that Kernberg is a strong advocate of
explicitly supportive psychodynamic therapy (SPT) as well as of more
exploratory dynamic therapy. In keeping with his emphasis on precise
diagnosis and the interface between diagnosis and the specific circumstances of the patient, his position is that supportive therapy may be in-
dicated when circumstances do not allow for exploratory therapy and/
or when the goals of therapy do not include change in psychological
structure, and when a patient's reality testing is impaired to the degree
that they fall into the psychotic range of personality organization.

Years after the Menninger study, when Kernberg's Personality Disorders Institute (PDI) at the Weill Cornell Medical College obtained
funding to carry out a randomized control trial involving TFP in 1999.
Kernberg, in keeping with his reading of the Menninger Research
Project, insisted on including an SPT cell in the study along with the
TFP cell and the dialectical behavior therapy (DBT) cell. This position reflected Kernberg's ongoing interest in the question that attracted
his attention since the Menninger study. While the trend in psychodynamic psychotherapy was a hybrid "supportive-expressive" approach,
Kernberg maintained the position that a clear distinction between the
two optimized clinical care. Indirect support for this view came later
from Per Høglend's research findings that lower-level patients do better in therapy that includes transference interpretations than in psychodynamic therapy without transference interpretation (Høglend et al.,
2008). Kernberg's decision to pursue the study of this distinction may
not have been in line with a mental health world in which cognitive-
behavioral therapies were increasingly popular in contrast to psychodynamic therapies and a more pragmatic approach might have included
only TFP and DBT, which would have allowed for more power in the
statistical analysis of the data. Kernberg's position reflected his identity as a psychoanalytic academic, pursuing research to better understand the differential impacts of exploratory psychodynamic therapy
in contrast to SPT. In essence, he chose a research design that favored
his clinical academic interests over the "horse race" model of a randomized controlled trial (RCT) that tries to demonstrate the superiority of one model of treatment over another. The nature of Kernberg's
research has been to look beyond limited notions of outcome and to
consider specific domains of change and mechanisms of change.

Upon becoming medical director at the Westchester Division of
New York Hospital-Cornell Medical Center (which was subsequently

to become the New York Presbyterian Hospital – Weill Medical College of Cornell University), Kernberg began to put together the informal research team that eventually carried out the RCT mentioned above. He partnered with John Clarkin as research director and John Oldham as co-leader to start weekly meetings of the Borderline Study Group mentioned in Chapter 1.

The group set about to systematically study and further develop the psychodynamic therapy that Kernberg had described in a series of writings being as early as 1968 (Kernberg, 1968). The first book that summarized what was to become TFP was published in 1989 (Kernberg et al., 1989). When the group turned to research on this model, it proceeded systematically through the steps that are needed to study a treatment: (1) conceptualizing the pathology, with ongoing refinements to Kernberg's writings on BPD; (2) conceptualizing the treatment with pilot testing and articulating it in a manual; (3) training a group of therapists to adherence and competence; (4) systematic testing leading to an RCT; (5) investigating moderators and mediators; and (6) looking at the generalizability of the treatment to other settings.

Over the years, Kernberg and his group received substantial funding from various sources. The first grant, from the American Psychoanalytic Association in 1987, supported developing both a manual for psychoanalytic psychotherapy of patients with borderline personality disorder and instruments to rate therapist adherence to the model of therapy. Over the years, additional funding was obtained from the National Institute of Mental Health (one grant awarded to Dr. Clarkin as principal investigator (PI) and one to Dr. Levy as PI), the DeWitt Wallace Readers Digest Foundation (Dr. Kernberg as PI), the Köhler Foundation (Dr. Levy as PI), the Weill Medical College of Cornell University Department of Psychiatry, the International Psychoanalytic Association (several with Dr. Levy as PI and one with Dr. Diamond as PI), the Borderline Personality Disorder Research Foundation (BP-DRF; Drs. Kernberg and Clarkin were PIs in the initial grant and Drs. Clarkin and Levy in a second and third grant), the American Psychoanalytic Association (Dr. Levy as PI), and the Dworman Foundation (Dr. Clarkin as PI). The initial grants funded developmental and pilot projects, leading up to the large grant from the BPDRF that funded the Personality Disorders Institute's RCT (Clarkin et al., 2007; Levy et al., 2006a) mentioned above and other grants that provided supplements to expand the study of the data from PDI RCT. The source of the BPDRF grant was an anonymous family whose life had been affected by BPD.

A representative of the family initially evaluated the most important sites that the Foundation found to be dedicated to helping patients with BPD, including Thomas McGlashan's group at Yale and John Gunderson's group at Harvard's McLean Hospital before deciding to grant the major award to Kernberg at the PDI. The main findings of the RCT and the progression to more detailed studies will be discussed below.

The first step in psychotherapy research is a clear conceptualization of the condition that the therapy claims to treat. Kernberg had elaborated the structural model of understanding personality disorders in his writings in the 1970s and 1980s. That understanding of the pathology served as the foundation for the manualization of the treatment (Kernberg et al., 1989; Yeomans et al., 1992, 2015; Clarkin et al., 1999; Clarkin et al., 2006). While the idea of "manualizing" a psychoanalytic treatment was and, in many circles, continues to be controversial, Kernberg was concerned that the rich wisdom of the psychoanalytic tradition remains spread out over almost innumerable texts and that the field lacks a systematic description of the application of those techniques. The Kernberg Borderline Study group's effort at manualization was different from currently available cognitive behavioral therapy (CBT) manuals. The group's first 1989 text was, like subsequent more fully elaborated versions, "principle-driven": it described the systematic application of psychoanalytic principles and techniques in the treatment of patients with BPD, starting with a careful assessment, then moving on to establishing the frame of the treatment, and finally describing the systematic employment of psychoanalytic techniques themselves, as discussed in Chapter 4 of this book on the development of TFP. This manualization of the therapy corresponded to Kernberg's long-held and continuing goal of simplifying the organization and teaching of psychoanalytic techniques. He often expressed frustration that, without an organized description of the application of psychoanalytic techniques, the richness of the psychoanalytic literature on theory and technique tended to create a mystification of psychoanalysis and psychoanalytic techniques that presented an obstacle to their broad application.

In keeping with the flow of the clinical process and with Kernberg's emphasis on the need for accurate diagnosis to guide the application of treatment, an early research effort was an attempt to establish the reliability of Kernberg's form of diagnostic interview: the structural interview (Kernberg, 1981, 1984). The goal of this interview is to establish a full picture of the patient's pathology that encompasses both specific symptoms and the individual's psychological structure in terms of identity integration vs. diffusion, level of characteristic defense mechanisms, quality of reality testing, level of aggression, and nature of moral functioning. An excellent example of this interview is found in "The Symfora Tapes" (Dalewijk and van Luyn, 2005), a series of recorded diagnostic interviews that compares the work of seven master clinicians in the area of personality disorders: Kernberg, Salmon Akhtar, Arthur Friedman, Marsha Linehan, Lawrence Rockland, Lorna Smith-Benjamin, and Michael Stone. While Kernberg's structural interview is a rich clinical instrument, investigators in the PDI group found that clinicians had difficulty establishing reliability with this interview. Consequently, a group within the team set out to develop and study the Structured Interview for Personality Organization (STIPO; Clarkin et al., 2004; Clarkin et al., 2017) that has become important both as a clinical diagnostic tool and as a research tool. Kernberg's contribution of items to this structured clinical interview introduced the clinical thinking that was embodied in the more open-ended structural interview. It is worth noting that the terminology can be confusing since the "structural interview" is so named because its goal is to establish an understanding of the patient's internal psychological structure (in terms of identity integration vs. diffusion, characteristic level of defense mechanisms, quality of object relations, level of internal aggression, and quality of reality testing, interpersonal relations, and moral functioning) and not because the interview itself is highly structured.

As the PDI group's research moved beyond the diagnostic phase to the therapy, an important step in the effort to fully understand and study the model of therapy was viewing videorecorded sessions. At that time, in the 1990s, recording sessions was considered a radical idea and met much resistance in analytic circles. Subsequently, it has become more widely accepted and, indeed, can be considered essential in evaluating therapeutic work since the affective state and nonverbal communication of both the patient and the therapist can be as important, or even more important, than the verbal content of the communication. The research team had anticipated patients might be reluctant to have their sessions recorded. Interestingly, some therapists showed more resistance to recording than patients. It was essential to move beyond this resistance since a frequent criticism of psychoanalytic work was that, even though analytic therapists were taught a relatively coherent model of treatment, it was impossible to know exactly what they did in sessions, with the risk that the application of analytical techniques varied widely in practice and, at times, may not reflect adherence to analytic principles.

Recording sessions allowed direct observation of the application of the treatment by the man who created it and who, now with the clinical research team, continued to develop and refine it. In observing the sessions, Kernberg would note instances when he felt he missed something or did not do well and would work with the team on how to modify and improve the application of technique. Other members of the research group sometimes noticed elements of Kernberg's interactions with patients that had not been described fully in his writings or that he said he did "naturally" without having described them. In particular, the videos demonstrated a type of work that, while adhering to technical neutrality, involved a style of verbal communication that was sometimes surprisingly natural and "human" in contrast to the somewhat intellectualized tone that often characterized his writings that could suggest the caricatured image of a psychoanalyst's coldly neutral interventions. Observation of the interactions was essential in displaying the importance of the nonverbal channel of communication and the atmosphere and tone in sessions. These were often quite different from what appeared in written transcriptions of sessions or process notes. Over time, these observations, along with the combined clinical experience of group members, led to an increased appreciation of the need to attend to containing and naming intense affect states before any effective interpretation could take place. It became clearer over time that clarification and confrontation, the first steps in the process of interpretation, were crucial elements in helping the patient observe the object relations dyads enacted in the treatment and their defensive function with respect to dissociated or projected experiences of the self and other – the major goal of interpretation in TFP. Recent research has supported this view (Kivity et al., 2021).

After clearly articulating the conceptualization of the pathology and the nature of the treatment, the next step was to see if the treatment described by Kernberg as a master clinician could be practiced by others in a way that was adherent and reliable in relation to the work of the model's creator. The video recordings were instrumental in assessing the work of those training in the model in terms of adherence and reliability. To operationalize the assessment, the PDI research group developed a rating instrument to evaluate therapists' adherence to the model of therapy, an instrument that the group continues to refine to better assess the therapist's work and to increase interrater reliability. In addition to being used in research, the instrument can be used during supervision sessions that include the therapist's discussion of developments in the therapy in conjunction with observation of a recorded session. On the global level, rating adherence involves rating the degree to which the therapist first attends to any elements of the treatment frame that might need to be addressed and then to the appropriateness of the application of the exploratory treatment techniques.

The year 1991, with the publication of Marsha Linehan's initial RCT of dialectical behavioral therapy (Linehan et al., 1991), was a watershed year in psychotherapy research. That study set an example and a new standard for psychotherapy outcome research. Especially in the United States, where cognitive-behavioral therapies had become increasingly popular and were becoming the mainstay of what was taught in psychology graduate schools, it was important to establish an evidence base for a model of therapy that could be part of a psychology curriculum. The psychoanalytic world, in general, was not well prepared for this situation. Linehan's initial study led to a series of studies of models of therapy for BPD that, while valuable, were somewhat limited in their scope by often being perceived as "horse races" that emphasized the results of the different therapies involved in the studies in terms of symptom change with little attention to the intervening variables (mediators and moderators) and the mechanisms of change involved in the therapies. In addition, the initial studies generally compared the model of treatment being studied to a weak and ill-defined "treatment-as-usual". One of the noteworthy features of the PDI's initial RCT was to study three well-defined and manualized treatment models, rather than using "treat-as-usual" as the comparison group.

Aware of the importance of establishing an evidence base and having articulated the model of treatment and standardized its teaching, the PDI research group went on to carry out a noncontrolled outcome study that followed two prior studies done by Mexican colleagues (Cuevas et al., 2000; López et al., 2004). The first PDI study used a "pre/post" design on a sample of patients, comparing patient variables at the end of one year of treatment to data on the patients' symptoms and functioning during the year prior to the initiation of treatment (Clarkin et al., 2001). This pilot study showed promising results. In the study, 23 women who met DSM-IV criteria for BPD and who had at least two incidents of suicidal or self-injurious behavior in the previous year were selected for one year of TFP treatment. Their clinical condition at the end of the year of TFP was compared to their clinical condition during the year prior to the treatment. There were significant changes in a number of dimensions, including a significant decrease in the number of patients who made suicide attempts, in the average medical risk of parasuicidal acts, and there were significantly fewer emergency room visits, hospitalizations, and days hospitalized. In addition, there were significant changes in the BPD diagnosis in that, after 12 months of treatment, 52.9% of the subjects no longer met criteria for BPD. A long-standing problem in treating BPD patients was the well-documented dropout rate. Research by Gunderson et al. (1989) found that 67% of BPD patients dropped out of therapy within the first six months of treatment. The PDI study had a dropout rate of 20% over one year. It should be noted that in the initial diagnostic assessment, 70% of the patients in this study were diagnosed with comorbid BPD and narcissistic personality disorder (NPD) based on the criteria of the Structured Clinical Interview for DSM-IV Axis II Personality Disorders (First & Gibbon, 2004).

In addition to changes in symptoms and self-destructive behaviors, this pilot study found structural changes in the quality of attachment representations and the capacity for mentalization. This and subsequent studies used the Adult Attachment Interview (AAI; George et al., 1985) to assess the attachment representations of borderline patients and the way they change over the course of TFP since insecure attachment is one of the hallmarks of borderline conditions. The features of borderline attachments, including the unpredictable shifts between clinging and repudiation, intense idealization and scathing devaluation, terrors of abandonment and unilateral rejection of others, were conceptualized as sequelae of insecure attachment organization and as failures of reflective function (RF; Fonagy et al., 1991; Fonagy et al., 1997; Fonagy et al., 2002 Gunderson et al., 1996). Attachment was assessed with the AAI (George et al., 1985; Main et al., 2008), a semistructured interview whose questions are designed to assess mentalization in attachment relationships, designated as reflective functioning (Fonagy et al., 1997). The AAI was used as one method of assessing the way mental representations of attachment change over the course of TFP treatment. Indeed, in this pilot study, significant increases were found over one year of outpatient TFP treatment for the continuous measures of attachment (i.e., coherence), with the majority of the participants showing shifts from disorganized to organized forms of attachment (Diamond et al., 2003). The study also found significant changes in ratings of reflective functioning as well as significant changes in the developmental level of object relations as assessed on the Object Relations Inventory differentiation-relatedness scale (Blatt et al., 1976). A comprehensive description of the overall study and assessment procedures has been presented in other publications (Diamond et al., 1999, 2003; Levy et al., submitted).

After the encouraging results of the pilot study, Kernberg and the PDI team went on to the first RCT of TFP. As mentioned above, Kernberg's interest in the differential indications for and results of an exploratory psychodynamic approach in contrast to a supportive one led to a research design with three treatment cells. The 90 female patients with a DSM-III diagnosis of BPD in the study were randomly assigned to TFP (Clarkin et al., 1999), to SPT (Appelbaum, 2006; Carsky, 2013), or to DBT (Linehan, 1993). As in the pilot study, the project investigated the therapies over one year, even though most treatment of BPD patients in community clinical conditions continues for longer. Statistical analysis was based on individual growth curve analysis that looked at changes in symptoms and domains of functioning over time for each of the patients and for each treatment group. Results showed that the three treatment models were associated with significant change over multiple domains of functioning. However, only TFP and DBT were associated with a decrease in suicidality. In addition, only TFP was significantly associated with reduction in impulsivity, irritability, verbal and direct assault, and aggression. These results are consistent with TFP's underlying model of the pathology that emphasizes the role of unintegrated aggressive affects in the mind of patients with BPD.

Given Kernberg's interest in psychological change as well as symptom change and, in particular, in change in psychological structure, the RCT, like the pilot study, included the AAI in its battery of research instruments to assess underlying psychological variables. In the absence of an instrument to directly assess identity integration, the most central concern in terms of psychological structure, the research team felt the AAI, based as it is on both the quality of descriptions of others and of self in relation to others and on the coherence of discourse in regard to early attachment relationships and experiences, could be considered a proxy for level of object relations and the degree of identity integration (Main, 1991; Buchheim & Diamond, 2018; Diamond et al., 2023). After one year of treatment, patients in the TFP cell of the study were significantly more likely than patients in the DBT or SPT cells to move from an insecure to a secure attachment style, to have increased attachment coherence, and to have increased reflective functioning (capacity for mentalization) in attachment relationships (Levy et al., 2006a). These findings were in line with the proposed mechanism of change in TFP: that encouraging reflection on affect states as they are experienced in the moment with the therapist is associated with an increase in RF and a related capacity to contain affects through language and then engage in reflection on contradictory affect states. This process of increased reflective capacity is associated with modification of internal representations of self and other from simplistic and intense to complex and nuanced. This change in the quality of internal representations takes place as projected aspects of the self become integrated, leading to increased modulation of affects, which, in turn, supports further improvement in reflective capacity (Levy et al., 2006b).

The next important development in TFP research was carried out independently of Kernberg by European colleagues in Vienna and Munich under the leadership of Stephan Doering as the PI (Doering et al., 2010). That RCT randomly assigned 104 female patients diagnosed with BPD to one year of treatment with either TFP or therapists in the community who were experienced in treating personality disorders. Patients in the TFP arm of the study, in comparison with the other treatment cell, showed a significant reduction in BPD criteria, in suicide attempts, and in hospitalizations, and also showed more improvement in social and personality functioning. The European study, like the PDI study, found that the patients treated with TFP were more likely to move from an insecure to a secure, and from a disorganized to an organized internal working model of attachment, to have increased attachment coherence, and to have an increased capacity for reflective functioning (Buchheim and Diamond, 2018). In addition, the European study found that patients receiving TFP showed more improvement in personality organization, as measured on the STIPO, than patients treated by experienced community therapists. This supported the view that TFP helps patients both at the level of symptoms and at the level of personality organization. In addition, the study found a relation between improvement in personality organization and symptomatic improvement.

A common misconception of psychodynamic psychotherapy is that it helps most with patients who are "psychologically-minded" or, in more current terminology, who have the capacity for mentalization/RF. In light of that misconception, it is important to note that the patients in the three treatment modalities in the PDI RCT all began treatment with similarly low levels of RF. In addition, analysis of the data showed that patients with low RF were less likely to drop out of TFP than to drop out of the other treatments (Levy, presentation, 2008). A hypothesis to explain this is that TFP, rather than being the abstract and intellectualized exercise in proposing interpretations that is sometimes the caricatured view of transference analysis, actually stays very close to the patient's experience in the moment and, consequently, can engage patients with low RF by focusing on the experience that is being shared, albeit sometimes perceived differently, by the patient and the therapist. In short, TFP, especially in its early phase, works with the concrete present experience rather than hypotheses about the past.

Kernberg's support of research at the PDI has had a multiplier effect. Based on the group's clinical experience that patients with combined narcissistic and borderline pathology posed unique treatment challenges and comprised 10%–70% of the patients in the research studies, further analysis investigated patterns of attachment and mentalization in this subgroup of patients. Study of the combined data from two RCTs (the New York–Cornell PDI RCT (Clarkin et al., 2007) and the Vienna–Munich RCT (Doering et al., 2010)) allowed for a more fine-grained exploration of the attachment representations of those with narcissistic and borderline pathology, how they might differ from patients with BPD without narcissistic pathology, and how they might change over the course of TFP. As expected, the two groups showed similar deficits in RF but somewhat divergent attachment representations. Patients with combined NPD/BPD were significantly more likely to be classified as dismissing (characterized by idealization/devaluation of others and dismissal of need for closeness) or cannot classify (characterized by oscillation between angry preoccupation or passive enmeshment with attachment figures and dismissing devaluation of them) than patients with BPD alone. The BPD group was significantly more likely to be classified as preoccupied (angrily or passively enmeshed with attachment figures) or unresolved (breakdown of discourse and reasoning in response to questions about loss and trauma) than was the NPD/BPD group (Diamond et al., 2013, 2014b). Thus, both clinical groups showed evidence of insecure and/or disorganized attachment representations, but in the NPD/BPD group this took the form of oscillation between opposing states of mind with respect to attachment relationships – most typically between dismissing and preoccupied discourse states of mind – while in the BPD group there was a more severe but focal breakdown in the monitoring of reasoning and discourse in response to specific questions about loss and abuse. This study provides validation for Kernberg's hypothesis that those with pathological narcissism are invested in a pathological grandiose self-structure – an internal world composed of highly idealized representations of self from which devalued representations are projected, with consequent fluctuations in self-esteem and affect dysregulation in the form of angry outbursts, emotional withdrawal, or detachment from others when needs for narcissistic self enhancement are not met. They may present the illusion of an integrated stable self but at the cost of greater pathology of relatedness.

Further investigations by an Israeli researcher include a detailed process study that examined the use of a specific therapy techniques in early-, middle-, and late-phase sessions of TFP, DBT, and SPT (Kivity et al., 2021). Therapist- and patient-speaking segments were rated for invitations on the part of the therapist for the patient to reflect on their mental state in the moment. These "bids for reflection" roughly correspond to the TFP techniques of clarification and confrontation. Patients' responses were rated for reflective functioning and acoustically encoded for affective arousal. The study found that bids for reflection were twice as common in TFP as in DBT and SPT and that the associated improvement in RF predicted lower emotional arousal.

Another line of research related to the model of the mind underlying TFP has to do with social cognition studies that provide indirect support to Kernberg's object relations view of the split internal world as the basis for borderline pathology. Central to this model is the idea that internal psychological conflicts around aggressive and libidinal affects are connected to internal representations of self and others that interfere with an accurate appraisal of external reality. This idea goes back to Kernberg's early book *Internal World and External Reality* (Kernberg, 1980). The splitting between the segments of the mind carrying negative affects and positive affects is extreme to the extent that a positive representation of self or other must be flawless and ideal to be associated with any positive feeling. Any experience of self or other that falls short of perfect switches over to the negative segment with a corresponding sense of disappointment and a cascade of negative affects (e.g., resentment, anger, hatred). This understanding of the Kleinian paranoid-schizoid organization has received some empirical support from studies in social cognition. Earlier studies had documented BPD patients' tendency to perceive neutral facial expressions as negative (Donegan et al., 2003). Subsequent work showed that a discrepancy between one's desired state and the circumstances encountered in a situation provokes negative affect states with a cascade of neurophysiological responses including fight-flight responses (Huprich et al., 2017). The challenge to the mind in such situations is to decrease the mismatch between the desired state and the current circumstances. The difficulty that BPD patients have with this challenge is understood as related to the extreme nature of the desired state as embodied in extreme internal representations of self and other, particularly (1) the wish to be cared for by an ideal caretaker and (2) difficulty in "owning" the negative affects activated by frustration in not finding the ideal caretaker and the related projection of these affects onto others that makes approaching others fraught with perceived risk. In simple terms, the rejection sensitivity that is frequently observed in BPD patients can be understood in terms of internal object representations. Fertuck, a senior member of the PDI, and colleagues found a tendency in BPD patients to not see trustworthiness in others and to perceive neutral facial expressions as negative (Fertuck et al., 2013). More recently, DePanifilis, a member of the PDI's Italian affiliate, has been shown that patients with BPD react to others' fair and accepting behavior as if it were unfair, frequently responding with hostile attitudes (DePanfilis et al., 2019). The authors of that study propose that the hostile attitudes observed are related to the discrepancy between the fair but imperfect experience of the other in the research conditions and the wish for a perfect other.

Venturing into the area of neurobiology, a pilot study carried out after the PDI RCT included looking at brain changes in BPD patients receiving TFP (Perez et al., 2016). The study looked at a cohort of ten female patients with a diagnosis of BPD. Functional magnetic resonance imaging (fMRI) before treatment and after one year of treatment showed decreased activation in areas of the brain associated with emotional reactivity and increased activation in areas of the brain associated with emotional and cognitive control as would be predicted by the TFP model of therapeutic action. Kernberg's interest in expanding our understanding of the role of neurobiology in personality disorders is reflected in his current dialogue with Mark Solms, particularly around drive and affect theory.

A more complete description of research related to Kernberg's model of object relations theory and to TFP can be found in Clarkin et al. (2023).

Beyond Kernberg's work with the PDI's research team and its affiliates in the International Society for TFP, Kernberg has been a long-standing advocate for an increased role of research in psychoanalysis in other settings. During his tenure as president of the International Psychoanalytic Association (1997–2001), he started that organization's Research Training Program (RTC). Peter Fonagy was the first director of the program, soon to be joined by John Clarkin as co-director. The group continues to have annual meetings that serve an important role in helping young researchers develop projects related to psychoanalysis. In addition, members of the PDI regularly present ongoing research at meetings of the American Psychoanalytic Association and regional and international organizations dedicated to the study of personality disorders.

In reviewing Kernberg's support of research, we are reminded of his commitment to advance both our understanding of psychoanalytic theory and technique, as it is continually enriched by developments in the field, and our understanding of the nature of personality disorders and how to help those who suffer from them. Many research opportunities await in terms of studying TFP beyond its application to female patients with a DSM BPD diagnosis to examine its effectiveness across a broader range of personality pathology and broader demographic group.

Chapter 6

Pathological Narcissism and Love Relations

Otto Kernberg's (1995, 2011, 2018) work in the area of love relations has been groundbreaking. Freud (1923/1961, p. 251) talked about love (e.g., the capacity to experience pleasure) and work (e.g., the capacity for efficient and productive activity) as the two anchors of psychological health. While most psychoanalytic thinkers from Freud on agree that pathology of love relations is an essential aspect of psychopathology, few have traced the developmental trajectory associated with normal and pathological love relations. In this chapter, we will describe Kernberg's views on the impact of pathological narcissism on love relations, including a description of the typical difficulties and distortions in the capacity to love found in those with narcissistic pathology and the developmental roots of such distortions. Combining neurobiology and psychoanalytic developmental theories in a joint conceptual framework, Kernberg traces how mature love relations evolve from the dawning of love and sensuality in early attachment relationships; develop through the experience of erotic excitement, rivalry, and aggression stimulated by oedipal development; progress through adolescent sexual and relational experimentation; and, with the consolidation of identity, reach mature forms in early to mid-adulthood with the integration of sexuality and attachment, love and tenderness.

Prophetically Freud (1914/1957, p. 88) wrote, "We must begin to love in order not to fall ill, and we are bound to fall ill, if, in consequence of frustration, we are unable to love." Freud identified narcissism as one strand in the trajectory of development that may turn pathogenic if it is developmentally prolonged as a result of frustration or fixation; but Freud had only a rudimentary understanding of the distortions in the representational world of self and object relations that might predispose one to narcissistic pathology of love relations.

DOI: 10.4324/9781003053415-6

While Freud's metapsychology of narcissism as a developmental stage has been challenged by much of contemporary infant research, his conceptualization of narcissism as it applies to love relations remains relevant. He identified two types of love: anaclitic (e.g., love for a cherished attachment figure experienced as separate from self) and narcissistic (e.g., love for another who represents an aspect of the self, i.e., what he is or once was or aspires to be). Foreshadowing object relations theory, Freud believed that in a mature love relation, anaclitic and narcissistic elements are intertwined. In this regard, Kernberg takes up where Freud left off. Based on a model of contemporary object relations theory, Kernberg recognized that these two modes of love are interwoven, so "the investment of objects and the investment of the self in the gratifying relations with such objects go hand in hand" (Kernberg, 1975a, p. 323). In intimate relationships, the object is always loved for both their unique otherness and capacity to enhance the self. In a mature love relation, loving the partner enhances self-love and self-love is also expanded by giving to one's partner.

A brief overview of Kernberg's developmental theory will further illuminate the trajectory of mature versus pathological love relations in those with narcissistic personality disorder (NPD). Kernberg (2022) amplifies Freud's dual drive theory of libido and aggression based on a model of contemporary object relations theory that combines neurobiology and psychoanalytic object relations theory in a joint conceptual system. While he maintains that unconscious conflicts between libidinal and aggressive drives are fundamental to an understanding of the dynamics and etiology of character pathology, including narcissistic pathology, he suggests that these drives are inextricably linked to and, in fact, organized by primary affect systems. Citing neurobiological evidence that is beyond the scope of this chapter, Kernberg (2018) suggests that affect systems are the primary motivators of human behavior in that they activate behaviors that ensure survival as well as define the contours of subjective experience (Kernberg, 2018). Amplifying Panksepp's (Panksepp & Biven, 2012) affect theory with psychoanalytic drive theory, Kernberg hypothesizes two major affect systems: a positive affiliative system of eroticism, attachment, and play bonding that jointly determine what Freud considered as the libidinal drive and, in contrast, a negative affect system of fight, flight, aggression, and separation/panic that jointly determine what Freud consistently considered as the aggressive drive, which functions to fight against or escape from attacks or dangerous situations. In addition, Kernberg, following Panksepp, Solms, and others, adds the seeking affect system, another generalized affect system that involves exploration which serves to reinforce the approach to gratifying experiences or situations. Kernberg conceptualizes these affect systems as drives in that they reflect the demands of the body on the psychic activity of the mind. In fact, in Kernberg's view, libido and aggression have emerged as the developmentally supraordinate integration of these affect systems. In this view, attachment or the proclivity for care seeking and caregiving, libido or sexual desire, and play bonding are basic drives that comprise the core of the positive affect system. Attachment is a primary motivational system that is fundamental to the capacity for developing and sustaining affectional bonds. It ensures survival in that it involves the seeking out of a primary caregiver in times of danger or threat and involves the capacity to depend on and to care for others. In this regard, attachment is a crucial component of love, together with eroticism and the affiliative system represented by play bonding. However, in Kernberg's view, human sexuality is a unique combination of eroticism, attachment, and play bonding that also involves an imaginative and transcendent or spiritual dimension.

Sexual arousal is not only an affect expression but also derives from specific mental scenarios (love maps) that are fundamental in generating erotic excitement, selection of sexual objects, masturbatory fantasies, physical desire, and paraphilic interests. Further, Kernberg has been influenced by Bataille's (1986) differentiation between the reproductive system, which involves sexual activity and erotic activity or eroticism, and a component of human sexuality that has spiritual, sacramental, and representational dimensions that may be linked to experiences of ecstasy, merger, violence, excess, and/or death. Kernberg observes that, in fact, attachment, which has to do with protection, safety, and care in the face of threat, may restrict this aspect of sexual experience. In addition, following Laplanche (1997), Kernberg stresses how through unconscious, inchoate mother-infant interactions, the mother communicates her own erotic imagination to the infant, thereby helping to structure the infant's own unconscious. The motivational systems described above determine the nature of the mother-infant affective bonds, which are then internalized under the condition of peak affect states in the form of dyadic units composed of representations of self in relation to others linked by a dominant affect. Under normal conditions, positive libidinal affect systems predominate, leading to the consolidation of an integrated and secure self in relation to an integrated positive concept of the other. Over the course of development, the major positive and negative motivational systems of libido and aggression and their respective affect systems become organized at a higher level of integration. It should be noted that the representational world is comprised of experiences of dyadic self-object-affect units stemming from the multiple motivational systems described above as they are activated at different points in development. However, the libidinal and aggressive systems, which reflect the supra ordinated integrations of all the positive and negative affect systems, play a key role in structuring conflicts and their resolution or lack of it through each developmental stage, with such conflicts encapsulated in unintegrated mental representations of self and other.

Kernberg hypothesizes that early wishes for merger, the experience of oneness with primary caregivers along with recognition of separateness, and early experiences of sensual delight that evolve through playful interactions are basic aspects of preoedipal dynamics that, although superseded by other developmental experiences, persist in the psyche enriching the later experience of love relations in normative development. However, under conditions of inordinate frustration, which can include intrusive, seductive, tantalizing, or frightening behavior short of actual physical maltreatment, as well as more severe forms of abuse and neglect, there may be severe disruption of early mother-infant attachment. In such cases, frustration generates aggression that cannot be integrated. Indeed, the intensity of aggression determines the need to protect the positive representationsof self and others by means of idealization as a defense against the frightening aggressive aspects that disrupt the relationship. Secure attachment involves the development of an integrated self (i.e., a self that can experience and flexibly integrate the full range of positive and negative emotions) relating to an integrated object representation under the sway of positive affect while, in contrast, insecure attachment involves a splitting off of aggression and a defensive idealization of the attachment figure as a defense against the disruption of the relationship. In the face of disruptive early experience, there is the development of excessive idealization that is split off from excessive aggression, leading to contradictory polarized experiences of self and other that may rapidly shift from one extreme to another or may become fixed in either the positive or the negative pole of the object relation. When this is the case, the result will be insecure attachment, in which the individual either alternately clings to or repudiates the attachment figure (anxious-ambivalent) or repudiates emotional contact with the other and becomes prematurely self-reliant (avoidant). In more severe cases, where there is a multigenerational legacy of maltreatment or trauma leading to actual abuse or to more subtle forms of maltreatment such as emotional unavailability, seductiveness, or frightening or frightened behavior on the part of the parent, the child may not be able to develop any consistent organized attachment strategy. The result is disorganization of the attachment system (Hesse & Main, 2006).

In the case of those who develop narcissistic pathology, the mother's incapacity to provide consistent love and care is replaced by her proclivity to provide admiration for the child's talents and capacities and often to treat the child as an extension of the self. In fact, Kernberg was the first to note that narcissistic pathology devolves from several parent-child relational patterns: for instance, parental overinvolvement and valorization of the child's attributes (often unusual talents or physical or intellectual characteristics) and exploitation of the child to feed the parent's own thwarted narcissism combined with cold, rejecting parental attitudes when the child fails to do so (Kernberg, 1975; Otway & Vignoles, 2006). In addition, in the histories of those with narcissistic pathology, there is a link between maltreatment, including abuse and neglect, and particularly emotional abuse (Hoglund, 1996; Johnson et al., 2001; Afif et al., 2011; Cater et al., 2011; Cohen et al., 2012; Maxwell & Huprich, 2014; Ensink et al., 2017).

These early developmental factors are only one vector that leads to the development of the *pathological grandiose self* in which all ideal, positive attributes are contained in the self, and all weaknesses and deficiencies are projected onto others who are systematically devalued. Kernberg, along with Bowlby (1980), has observed that those with narcissistic pathology tend to have insecure avoidant or dismissing attachment in which there is either active derogating dismissal or brittle idealization of attachment relationships, a valorization of personal strengths and autonomy, and a cool contemptuous attitude towards attachment figures who are seen as inferior or contemptible. Those with avoidant dismissing attachment tend to have two conflicting sets of representations: a dominant model of self as superior and autonomous in relation to idealized or devalued others, and the other model, which is dissociated and/or not consciously available, based on experiences of rejection or lack of care of a vulnerable self in relation to an emotionally unavailable and rejecting other who may be defensively idealized. In fact, several studies have now affirmed that those with narcissistic pathology are likely to have insecure avoidant/dismissing attachment or disorganized attachment, in which they oscillate between insecure avoidant and anxious ambivalent-attachment states of mind (Diamond et al., 2014a). Speaking to Kernberg's view that attachment and sexuality are two intertwined behavioral systems, both of which contribute to the nature of mature love relations, there are considerable research findings linking attachment status to the nature of sexual relationships. Those with secure attachment have a propensity to value and commit to long-term sexual/romantic relationships, to show mutuality and satisfaction in sexual relationships, and to integrate affection, tenderness, and sexuality. Those with dismissing/avoidant attachment report experiencing sexual pleasure, but have a tendency to use sex to control others, to focus on their own sexual prowess, and to curtail intimacy and maintain emotional distance; while those with preoccupied/anxious attachment fear abandonment, subordinate their own sexual needs and desires in the quest for closeness, and idealize others whom they experience as if they are part of the self (Mikulincer & Shaver, 2007; Carrasco, 2013).

It should be noted that for those with narcissistic pathology, idealization, which is a normal component of both attachment and the erotic systems, becomes defensively inflated and split-off. When the early attachment figures are disappointing or exploitative, there may be excessive and premature internalization of object relationships at the expense of the development of actual interpersonal relationships with the caregivers, who are inordinately idealized to counter the recognition of their inadequacies. Such idealization predisposes to the development of an insecure attachment relationship, which is then transferred from mother to father in the oedipal passage.

This idealization, combined with the projection of the negative affects, distorts the oedipal relation for those with pathological narcissism in several ways. Under conditions of insecure attachment to the mother, the relationship to the father may function as compensatory providing another pathway to secure attachment. However, conflicts around oedipal desire and prohibitions, as well as rivalry and guilt, may lead to further deterioration of attachment security. There may be excessive inhibition or premature activation of the erotic system, leading to problems with the integration of attachment, sexual excitement, erotic desire, and aggression – all components of a mature love relation that depend, to some extent, on the successful resolution of the oedipal passage. In those with narcissistic pathology, oedipal resolution is impeded by an intolerance for thirdness, that is, the inability to tolerate exclusion from the dyadic intimacy of the parental couple. The child in the oedipal situation must be able to imagine being the excluded third in relation to the parental couple as well as being the love object (in fantasy) of one parent who stimulates erotic excitement, while being the competitor of the other parent who is relegated to the role of rival. The individual with pathological narcissism or narcissistic personality disorder is often unable to integrate these multiple psychic positions involving disparate representations of parents as loved attachment figures, desired oedipal objects, and dreaded rivals, and the varied representations of self in relation to others that are linked to them. The experience of such variable perspectives on self and other fosters the integration of the representations of the parents, shoring up the distinction between fantasy and reality, as well as the integration of love and hatred, since the parents who are actual attachment figures are also in fantasy the object of intense love and hatred. Such an integration leads to the emergence of the depressive position (Klein, 1946, 1957), which involves taking responsibility for one's own negative feelings of envy, anger and hatred, guilt and remorse about the impact of these feelings on others, and desires to make reparation to the loved objects who may have been harmed in fantasy or reality by the self (Britton, 1992, 2004). In the case of individuals with narcissistic pathology, such integration is not possible. Instead, the narcissistic individual strives to remain forever at the apex of the oedipal triangle: they are perpetually connected with conflicted desire and longing for exclusive possession of the idealized, unattainable oedipal object; perpetually seeking admiration from an idealized rival or competitor; and perpetually locked into a rivalrous struggle with such a competitor. One such narcissistic individual, for example, could only sustain sexual interest in a partner if he continually imagined himself as the object of admiration and envy by an idealized rival.

The persistence of oedipal illusions of union with unattainable objects is another configuration of oedipal fixation in individuals with pathological narcissism and/or NPD. An example is a relatively high-functioning female journalist with narcissistic personality disorder who remained fixated on a relationship with a colleague she had met on assignment ten years previously and with whom she had had a brief affair. The relationship continued without any definitive commitment, and, although she saw him only intermittently, she persisted in the illusion that he was the only man she could love and that this feeling was reciprocated, despite the fact that he lived in another continent, visited her infrequently, and made no commitments. The therapist's attempts to explore the tenacious nature of these illusions and how they curtailed her potential to form a relationship in the present that might, in fact, lead to an enduring commitment were met with scathing attacks. It was only when the therapist began to explore how this illusory relationship, in fact, also limited her engagement in therapy that she began to understand the meaning of this oedipal illusion. Far from expressing a great passion for another, this illusory relationship was fueled by narcissistic illusions of perfection, self-sufficiency, and emotional remoteness that, in fact, curtailed and constricted her relational possibilities.

Another typical manifestation of oedipal conflicts characteristic of narcissistic pathology involves the pattern that Kernberg (1995) refers to as "reverse triangulation" in which the narcissistic individual splits the image of the other into the parental (maternal or paternal) nonerotic partner and the devalued, erotically exciting lover, thereby preserving their position as the child in an oedipal triangle where they remain the object of adoration and desire and competition between the two parents. Such a scenario differs from the typical oedipal scenario in terms of both the depth of the split between the valorized, asexual object and the devalued erotically exciting object, and in the somewhat infantile, dependent nature of the relationship with both love objects. The individual is unable to engage in depth or sustain a long-term commitment, maintaining attitudes of entitlement and exploitativeness towards both love objects (Kernberg, 1995). In situations where narcissistic individuals are involved with multiple relationships that are kept secret from the primary partner, there are often underlying fears of abandonment and inhibitions towards deepening any relationship.

It should be noted that in patterns such as reverse triangulation Kernberg sees residues of preoedipal wishes for merger, of exhibitionism in the sense of being a desired object for multiple mother figures, and of voyeurism in the form of wanting knowledge of parent's intimate sexual life, along with oedipal dynamics of rivalry and competition with father or mother, involving the desire to take revenge on women or men by making them compete for them. Such fantasies may take both heterosexual and homosexual directions depending on the sexual orientation and gender identity of the individual involved. In Kernberg's view, one of the distinguishing features of sexual passion and eroticism are the polymorphous perverse fantasies and practices and the extent to which they are integrated as opposed to repressed or split-off in mature love relations to the enrichment of the couple's sexual life. Kernberg (1995, 2018) affirms that healthy love relations may take homosexual or heterosexual forms depending on constitutional, environmental, cultural, and developmental factors. As he put it recently,

> I have no problem with whatever the sexual behavior is, I'm interested in the extent to which there is a capacity for mature love relation as I tried to define it and to what extent there isn't, and to what extent not having such a relationship is experienced as a problem.
>
> (Kernberg, 2023)

In Kernberg's view then, a mature love relation involves the integration of sexual excitement with enduring attachment, erotic strivings with tenderness, ongoing mature idealization as opposed to unrealistic defensive or primitive idealization of the partner, and the sense of fulfilment of the need to depend on and care for another. Perhaps most importantly, it involves the psychological capacity to see and cherish the other as a unique and separate individual rather than as an extension of or complement to the self. Throughout the life span, people without pathological narcissism can expand their love of others predicated on a deep and enduring investment in a passionate connection to the other who is appreciated for their own unique qualities and characteristics. Such a state of mutuality and reciprocal relatedness required for a mature love relation is clearly antithetical to the inability of individuals with pathological narcissism to accept aspects of the partner that fail to enhance the self, to become emotionally dependent on another person, or to sustain emotional investment in an intimate relationship beyond the gratification of immediate dependent and sexual needs.

Instead, individuals with narcissistic pathology suffer from feeling that to depend emotionally on another person represents a loss or diminishment of their own greatness. Needing another person generates intense envy and evokes feelings of vulnerability and inferiority to the needed and potentially superior person. As a result, the unconscious tendency to devalue the partner as well as their own needs for attachment and dependency erodes the feelings of love and intimacy and tends to dissipate the sexual excitement in intimate passionate relations. Unconscious envy leads to defensive spoiling of the "good" that is received from the person who was initially idealized, leaving the patient bored, empty, and resentful. The more disturbed the narcissistic individual, the more pronounced the narcissistic features, and the more negative affects, such as anger, hatred, and envy, will persist reflecting split-off areas of functioning that interfere with the integration of loving and hateful feelings so essential to mature love relations.

Individuals with pathological narcissism and/or narcissistic personality disorder (NPD) function along a broad spectrum of pathology. At the mildest level, patients with pathological narcissism and NPD give a surface presentation of functioning quite appropriately in the social realm, are able to carry out work and professional demands, and are able to be a partner in a stable, if superficial, love relation. However, in these higher functioning narcissistic individuals, conflicts show mostly glaringly in their intimate relations, in the subtle devaluation and contempt they show towards others in both their love and professional relationships, and in their endlessly unsatisfied ambitions and sense of emptiness that requires continuous external stimulation. Many such individuals have arranged their lives to procure the admiration and approval they crave so that their difficulties can be well disguised through compensatory grandiosity and an external appearance of satisfaction. With those who are higher functioning, narcissistic elements may predominate in love relations, but they may coexist with some capacity for affectional bonds, although relationships are likely to remain superficial and to privilege admiration over love. In contrast, in more disturbed narcissistic individuals, those who function at a lower borderline level, there is an incapacity to invest deeply in any love relation except transient sexual involvements, resulting in a defensive withdrawal from all intimate emotional and sexual relationships. In addition, more disturbed narcissistic individuals may be characterized by the shutting down of the capacity for sensual pleasure or sexual excitement, or a defensive investment in work to the exclusion of all deep relationships. For those with more severe narcissistic pathology, the narcissistic dimension may eclipse the anaclitic dimension altogether so that love relations are based on exploitation to gratify narcissistic needs.

At all levels of narcissistic pathology, however, careful evaluation of the individual's love life reveals significant problems. The basic dynamics of the narcissistic personality involve a struggle with intense conscious and unconscious conflicts around envy, oscillations between grandiosity and vulnerability and between sense of self-importance and self-aggrandizement, and bouts of self-doubt and inferiority, all of which are particularly stimulated in intimate relations with a sexual partner.

For those with pathological narcissism, there is investment not in relationships with others but in the pathological grandiose self. The pathological grandiose self is a sense of self that is comprised of positive aspects of the real self, idealized aspects of the self, and idealized aspects of others (Kernberg, 1975, 1977, 1984, 2021; Diamond et al., 2022). The pathological grandiose self involves splitting off and projecting onto others of any aspects of the self that cause pain, anxiety, shame, or other negative affects, which are experienced as intolerable, and the simultaneous incorporation, denial, or introjection of aspects of others that are perceived as unique or admired or that evoke envy. For higher functioning narcissistic individuals, this involves denial or avoidance of aspects of reality that don't affirm the grandiose self, or, in more extreme cases, near total, if episodic, avoidance of living in reality when the grandiose illusions that sustain the grandiose self, which is fundamentally a defense against feelings of inferiority and emptiness, are threatened. All of the above preclude genuine mature love. Others are loved not as unique and separate individuals but for their representation of idealized or devalued aspects of the self, or, particularly in more severely disturbed patients with narcissistic personality disorder, for being an idealized, powerful, and sometimes punitive internal object representation felt to be part of the self. Hence the structural development of a pathological grandiose self results in a typical failure to develop mature love relations and a deficit in the psychological capabilities involved in such relations.

Often those with narcissistic pathology functioning at a higher level will be successful at attracting romantic partners in short-term romantic contexts due to their investment in physical appearance and their need to be admired for their superficial characteristics and accomplishments. However, they tend to have relationships characterized by low levels of emotional intimacy, trust, warmth, and caring, and high levels of antagonism – all of which lead to difficulties in developing and sustaining long-term romantic relationships. In addition, research studies have shown that individuals with pathological narcissism report low levels of relationship satisfaction and low relationship quality (experienced by both partners). Not surprisingly, individuals with pathological narcissism are also more likely to be chronically unfaithful because they tend to show lower levels of commitment and investment in relationships. Interestingly, although infidelity is common, they may react with vengefulness and inability to forgive after transgressions by romantic partners (e.g., if the partner is unfaithful or devaluing), which speaks to the persistence of unresolved oedipal conflicts around rivalry and triangulation. Also, Kernberg has observed that some individuals with pathological narcissism do not experience feelings of jealousy in relation to their partners because to be jealous would involve acknowledging the value of the other and involve a level of investment they do not feel. Instead, they may feel flattered or triumphant if their partner is admired or desired by others, again speaking to the pattern of reverse triangulation in which they need to have an admired and admiring rival in the picture to sustain sexual interest in a partner. Kernberg's clinical portraits of the love relations of those with pathological narcissism delineated above have been affirmed by research by social and clinical psychologists (Campbell & Campbell, 2009; Carlson et al., 2011; Czarna et al., 2014).

Those with narcissistic pathology also tend to develop relationships that are exploitative and parasitic. Higher functioning narcissistic individuals may develop stable if shallow relationships with socially prominent persons and use the partner's accomplishments or social status to shore up their own grandiosity, either appropriating the partner's talents and achievements as their own or exploiting the partner by parasitic financial, social, and emotional dependency. Or they may form a relationship with someone far beneath their own socioeconomic status or educational level, which also paradoxically facilitates the stabilization of narcissistic grandiosity since the individual can constantly demonstrate their superiority in relation to the other. Such depreciated relationships may also satisfy the often covert sadomasochism, that frequently accompanies narcissistic pathology. In such relationships with depreciated others, the partner is really a servant or a convenient fixture, and devaluation and resentment are institutionalized in chronic hostile, devaluing behavior. At the same time, being with a depreciated partner may satisfy the need for punishment and humiliation – the self-critical aspect that often lurks under the grandiose surface.

In terms of sexual behavior, there may be a capacity to maintain a stable couple relationship but without the integration of attachment, tenderness, and sexual excitement. In fact, a search for dissociated sexual experiences as both a source of excitement and a replacement of intimacy may become prominent. Here we find the pattern of narcissistic patients who are socially isolated but pursue an intense involvement in "virtual sexual engagements" through the internet, spending much of their free time watching pornography, in interchange of erotic messages and/or involved in one-night stands. In other cases, the accommodation to narcissistic pathology takes the form of a life devoid of emotional engagement in a sexless relationship while intense sexual relationships are split off from the couplehood and expressed in temporary engagements with others, thus providing the conditions for the stability of the narcissistic individual's grandiosity. In such cases, there is a split between idealized but desexualized love objects who confer stability and sexually exciting love objects with whom there is little or no emotional involvement.

In more severely disturbed narcissistic patients, those with low borderline structure, the grandiose self's defense against a sense of the self as inferior and even shameful may involve a sense of superiority tied up with a powerful, punitive internal or external object experienced as an aspect of self. The dominant object relational dyad of such individuals is of a persecuted self in relation to an indifferent or sadistic other, with a linking affect of hatred or indifference. The individual may sustain a view of the self as exceptional, but the sense of the self as special is tied up with being unrelentingly bad or damaged, with the conviction that nothing or no one can or will alleviate the suffering. These are the individuals who frequently have negative therapeutic reactions manifesting as pleasure in destructiveness, including defeat of the therapist and the treatment, and in engagement in sadomasochistic relationships with dangerous, destructive, or self-destructive elements.

For more severely disturbed narcissistic patients, a central organizer of the pathological grandiose self, then, is subjugation to ideal, punitive internal objects with the sense of self being experienced as as isolated, shameful, and bad. The self is perpetually subject to persistent criticism from such powerful, punitive negative objects that are not experienced as separate from the self, a dynamic originally termed the "internal saboteur" by Fairbairn (1952). While outwardly such disturbed narcissistic patients may present as detached, hollow, empty, or depressed, in fact they are often preoccupied with grandiose fantasies of success, triumph, or omnipotence that eludes them in life. The individual is in perpetual search for the ideal or bad enough object to counter an underlying sense of desolation, isolation, shame, and unworthiness. Kernberg, along with Fairbairn, stipulates that the allure of such a formidable internal object is due to the fact that it is both frustrating and seductive or tantalizing. For the more disturbed narcissistic individual, an internal relationship with a rejecting or tantalizing internal object protects against dreaded failures in actual relatedness. Many such patients are unable to sustain any love relations, suffer from severe sexual inhibition, or engage in a series of transient sadomasochistic relationships with no commitment or depth.

By contrast, a mature love relation requires the potential for integration of attachment and sexual passion, the development of basic trust, and the capacity for dependency; the tolerance of ambivalence with the awareness of one's own capacity for hatred and aggression and the tolerance of such negative affects in the partner; the gratitude for the love received by a partner and interest in their life project; the development of a joint ego ideal, joint aspirations and joint life goals; and, above all, the capacity for mature interdependence and reciprocity (Kernberg, 2012). A mature love relation also involves containment of the paranoid mechanisms that emerge when the tolerance of negative emotional states and conflicts in a couple's life is being tested by adversity. The disappearance of prevalent mutual power struggles as an expression of the decrease of such paranoid tendencies and, very importantly, the repeated re-encounter of sexual passion as a permanent aspect of the relationship are important indicators of a couple's mature relation. It should be noted that reengagement in sexual passion can stem from the resuscitation of idealization of the partner that is often an important and necessary component of falling in love.

In conclusion, Kernberg reminds us that it is important to distinguish between pathological and mature idealization. The capacity for idealization of the love object is one of the characteristics of a mature adult love relation. Mature idealization is based on the capacity to maintain an idealized view of the body and person of the other that becomes the repository of the history of their love and sexual passion – while still seeing the other realistically. Such an idealized view of the other forms a wellspring for the renewal of the relationship throughout time, even in the face of aging and diminishment. Mature idealization is also based on shared values that provide a source of guiding ideals for the partners and a direction for joint projects and investments. In addition, mature idealization also preserves the capacity to maintain love and acceptance of the partner even in the face of aggression-laden interactions that are part of the inherent ambivalence of human relationships. If healthy, idealization can function as one factor that enables couples to contain aggression within the framework of love. In contrast, primitive idealization in those with narcissistic pathology functions as a defense against aggressive feelings towards the partner and can easily shift into devaluation and contempt. As such, it interferes with the integration of loving and hateful feelings that characterize all love relations.

In sum, Dr. Kernberg has stated that his interest in love relations was an extension of his work with patients with borderline and narcissistic personality disorders in whom he saw extreme and destructive love relations, including sadomasochistic and sadistic perversions. With narcissistic patients, he encountered a group with "the most severe incapacity to love" and

> to help such patients seems an exciting task. I used whatever I thought I was gaining in understanding to help some patients to really love who have not been able to do it before and being concerned about why the failure and why the success in different cases.
> (Kernberg, personal communication, July 21, 2023)

In addition, in his work with patients with neurotic disorders, Kernberg encountered mystifying and perplexing aspects of passion, which he believed had been undertheorized in psychoanalytic thought in the United States. He turned to French analysts, such as Laplancheand Bataille, by whom he was particularly influenced, going beyond the bounds of psychoanalytic theory to philosophy, the arts, literature, and theology to understand passionate love. He spent three months in Paris at the Paris Psychoanalytic Institute where he consulted with André Green, Denise Brunswig, Michelle Fain, and other analysts of the French school who were working in this area. He stated, "I was interested in the normal aspects of passion." He has stated that experiences in his own life and less than satisfactory experiences in his own analyses catalyzed his extended explorations in this area. In sum, Kernberg has made invaluable contributions to our understanding of love relations, both healthy and pathological, and in so doing has helped us to deepen our understanding of love's mysteries.

Chapter 7

Social and Political Perspectives on Narcissism and Its Disorders

Introduction

One of Otto Kernberg's unique contributions has been to call attention
to the complex relationship between collective and individual narcissism. Understanding narcissism through a clinical lens can grant us
perspective on those whose behavior is considered narcissistic by society at large and the ways narcissistic leaders may exploit and organize
the narcissistic strivings of ordinary citizens. From the publication of
his seminal work *Borderline Conditions and Pathological Narcissism*
in 1975 to his recent papers such as *Malignant Narcissism in Groups*
(Kernberg, 2020), Kernberg has defined the contours of pathological
narcissism (PN) as a complex and urgent mental disorder related to
significant interpersonal and occupational problems in individuals
which ramify into social and political life. With the emergence of narcissism as a both a clinical concept and a social phenomenon over the
past 50 years, the idea of a continuum between psychic health and
abnormality, originally formulated by Freud (1940/1964), has found
new centrality within psychoanalytic thought. Under Kernberg's leadership, members of the Personality Disorders Institute (PDI) have
explored the continuities and discontinuities between narcissism as a
social trend and narcissism as a clinical diagnosis. Kernberg has conceptualized narcissism and its disorders from a contemporary object
relations perspective in terms of distortions in the formation of the self
and its relation to others (objects), both internal and external; as such,
his conceptualization encompasses concepts related to self (identity,
self-esteem, and affect regulation), as well as interpersonal functioning (e.g., empathy and intimacy). At the same time, more than any
other psychoanalytic theorist, he has explored how narcissism, both

DOI: 10.4324/9781003053415-7

pathological and normal, has implications for social, political, and organizational life. Kernberg allows that narcissistic personality traits such as self-centeredness, self-aggrandizement, social dominance, self-importance, grandiosity, and attention-seeking are socioculturally sanctioned in our time and may lead to self-enhancing and self-promoting behaviors and attitudes in the general population. Yet Kernberg maintained the distinction between social or collective narcissism, or narcissistic personality traits, on the one hand, and narcissistic personality disorders (NPD) as a specific pathological structuring of the personality, on the other hand.

In this chapter, we will focus on several aspects of his work on the relationship between collective and individual narcissism including the following: (1) the continuities and discontinuities between narcissism as a clinical diagnosis and narcissism as a dominant personality trait in contemporary society; (2) the rise of malignant narcissistic leaders worldwide, who foster collective narcissism in the citizenry; and (3) the contributions of contemporary psychoanalytic object relations theory, particularly the theory of human motivation as a complex mesh of inborn affective dispositions that structure the drives of love and aggression and the way these find expression in interpersonal and social life.

Kernberg's interest in social and political aspects of personality disorders in general and NPD in particular has roots in his own experience of forced immigration from Vienna in the 1930s when the Nazis occupied Austria and he and his immediate family, along with many Jews and other ethnic minorities, were forced to flee to escape persecution and death. As a result of observing Vienna under the Nazi regime as well as perilous social developments in Chile and Argentina after his family emigrated to Latin America, he stated that exploring the "relationship between individual narcissistic pathology and social pathology came naturally to me" (Kernberg, 2021). As a result of these experiences, Kernberg developed an interest in group behavior and the conditions that might foster regression in ordinary citizens, even those without significant narcissistic and antisocial pathology, to corrupt their moral compass, surrender their sense of judgment, and alter their sense of identity to the extent that they engage in callous, even savage behavior. In fact, one of Kernberg's most important and original contributions has been to understand how, in times of political and social turmoil, malignant narcissistic leaders foster collective narcissism in the citizenry by promising the restoration of a tribal form of supremacy. This is often at the expense of demonized out-groups, rather than promoting a truthful and complex view of reality and humanistic ideals of individual autonomy, social responsibility, and equality. Observing firsthand how cognitive functions, including judgment, moral functioning, and autonomy, are reduced as individuals are swept into a mass movement under the influence of demagogic leaders has led Kernberg to study malignant narcissism and its treatment as part of the theory of severe personality disorders. Over the course of his long career, then, Dr. Kernberg has sought to understand the social dimension of conscious and unconscious functioning in individuals swept into a group regression under the sway of malignant narcissistic leaders. Moreover, he has increasingly concerned himself with what we can do preventively at both the individual and the societal level to short-circuit such regressive group processes. His work in this regard has become a beacon of enlightenment, hope, and resistance to the ominous social trend towards authoritarianism and tyranny that threatens the eclipse of democracy worldwide (Snyder, 2017; Applebaum, 2020).

In this regard, Kernberg has acknowledged that he has been indebted to several major theorists, including Christopher Lasch's work on the *Culture of Narcissism*, who himself was influenced by the work of Adorno (1967, 1968) and Horkheimer (Adorno and Horkheimer, 1944/1972) of the Frankfurt School, which developed in Germany during World War II and the postwar era. The theorists of the Frankfurt School identified the authoritarian personality as a dominant personality type, in which an inflated and empty self (consistent with narcissistic traits if not disorders) replaced a fully individuated and autonomous individual, fostering mindless identifications with and allegiance to totalitarian leaders (Adorno et al., 1950). Twenty years later, Lasch (1979) coined the term "the Culture of Narcissism" to describe the preoccupation with self-fulfillment over adherence to communal and family values that previously lent depth and continuity to personality, excessive individualism over concern for well-being of others, hedonism over self-discipline, and ruthless profit seeking over promotion of the social good in the corporate sector – all of which he identified as the characterological legacy of late-stage capitalist societies, as reflected in the typical American personality. Lasch saw the inflation of narcissistic traits, if not full-blown NPD, in the general populace as indicative of a sense of personal unmooring experienced in response to the economic stagnation and political turmoil of the 1970s, particularly the loss of American power on the international stage epitomized by the defeat in Vietnam. Lasch and other social theorists attribute the trend towards the inflation of narcissism in the contemporary personality to a variety of changes in our society and culture, including the breakdown of family structure and traditional social roles that challenge the process of identity formation; the spread of bureaucracy that reaches its tentacles into the sphere of private life, strangling individual initiative, and self-sufficiency; the cult of consumption or the tendency to commodify human experience, whereby investment in consumer goods and technological services replace investment in interpersonal relationships; and the array of media images that creates an image veil that substitutes stereotyped reflections for a genuine reflection of individual complexities (Adorno, 1967, 1968; Adorno & Horkheimer, 1944/1972; Lasch, 1979).

Continuities and Discontinuities between Individual and Collective Narcissism

While Kernberg (1975a) agrees that such social trends are part of a narcissistic culture, he hypothesizes that social alienation alone cannot in itself foster the self-estrangement and inner deterioration of object relations experienced by the narcissistic individual. This is because object relations refer not to actual interpersonal interactions but to the intrapsychic structures or mental representations of self and other that represent a mesh of drive, affect, developmental stage, defense, and also actual experience of early familial relationships. Rather, he has linked narcissistic pathology to an investment in a pathological self-structure, the pathological grandiose self. This self-structure is a compilation of real and idealized self-representations in which all that is good, ideal, and superior is encapsulated in the self, while all that is defective, weak, or inferior is projected onto others who are consequently devalued (Kernberg, 1975a, 1984, 1986, 2007). The pathological grandiose self may present the appearance of smooth and effective social functioning with few manifest symptoms; at best, it obscures episodic fluctuations of self-esteem and shallowness in understanding self and others, and, at worst, it causes severe, chronic problems with self-regard and a dismantling of relationships. Individuals with a pathological grandiose self lack the well-integrated and cohesive set of internalized self (and object) representations that provide depth and continuity to experience. However, the pathological grandiose self may meet the requirements of an industrial and technologically advanced society because it is stable enough to fit into the routinized, performance-oriented structure of work, but, lacking a cohesive and integrated core, the pathological grandiose self is easily manipulated by the mass media and bureaucratic institutions.

Kernberg rejects any direct correspondence between social trends characteristic of a narcissistic society and the subjective experience of emptiness and self-estrangement of those with pathological narcissism (PN) and NPD, but he does allow that certain character types (e.g., those with PN and NPD) will be more likely to embrace social trends seen as narcissistic. He observes that those with milder forms of narcissistic pathology may not only appear to be asymptomatic but may indeed embody those traits that guarantee success in contemporary society, particularly corporate and bureaucratic structures. According to Kernberg (1975), it is precisely the narcissistic personality's emptiness, lack of emotional depth, and lack of emotional investment in enduring intimate bonds that cause them to function optimally in certain "political and bureaucratic organizations in which lack of commitment means survival and access to the top" (p. 308). However, in Kernberg's view, this surface presentation is a façade that often masks either an enraged, needy individual who ruthlessly devalues others and what they have to offer in order to protect against underlying feelings of envy and worthlessness, or an inadequate, vulnerable individual who merges with idealized figures on whom they project their own covert grandiosity. Kernberg allows that a culture of narcissism may tolerate and even reward those with narcissistic traits and full-blown narcissistic disorders, particularly those who appear to fit seamlessly into leadership roles in media conglomerates, corporate jobs, or government positions in which they sustain their grandiose illusions through manipulating and dominating others. But a narcissistic culture does not in and of itself account for the underlying pathological organization of such individuals, which is the result of a confluence of constitutional, developmental, and familial/environmental influences (Diamond et al., 2022).

Over several generations, social trends like family uprootedness, social disorganization and dislocation, the bureaucratization of work, the stereotyped images offered by the mass media, and shifts in gender roles might eventually permeate the immediate relational world of the family, catalyzing changes in the intrapsychic structure of the child. For example, whereas narcissistic pathology in women used to be expressed through preoccupation with envy and being envied, and obsession with bodily perfection evident in inordinate concern with weight or looks (Kaplan, 1991), currently PN in women as well as men is likely to take the form of inability to commit to relationships in depth, ruthless exploitation of others in the interests of self-aggrandizement and advancement at work, and uncritical and seamless conformity to the empty and exploitative social practices and values often promulgated by corporate culture (Kernberg, personal communication, 2013). Interestingly, in their meta-analysis of college students' ratings on the Narcissistic Personality Inventory (NPI), Twenge and colleagues (2008) found that sex differences in narcissistic personality traits have decreased substantially, with increases in narcissistic traits among women now comparable to that of men – a research finding that affirms this clinical observation. The traits included both adaptive traits such, as self-sufficiency and agency, and maladaptive traits, such as exploitativeness and entitlement.

Kernberg (1989) has also explored the ways in which certain aspects of mass culture, with its array of banal and stereotyped images, stunt the development in the domains of self- and interpersonal functioning (ego development) and moral functioning (superego development). Specifically, he hypothesizes that increasingly in normative groups, the development of moral values shows the imprint of latency age functioning, including rigid, simplistic morality that privileges slavish adherence to conventional norms of good and evil, and the tendency to submerge individual identity in group norms. These aspects of latency age functioning that are fostered by aspects of mass culture interfere with maturation, including psychosexual and object relations development. The result is a proneness to regression in the individual personality to aspects of latency age functioning, with failures to integrate genital sexuality with polymorphous perverse inclinations and to blend tenderness with sexuality in ways that temper aggression, in the submersion of eroticism in aggression at the group level or its blunting in the interests of cultural conformity and mass consumption, and, finally, in the linking of sex with excretory functions. These trends are evident in the crude exhibitionism and bathroom humor of some contemporary young adult films and television shows. Also contributing to the proneness to regression and failure of psychosexual and object relations development is the fact that the latency age period itself has become shorter so that children do not have a chance to mature emotionally before they encounter a highly sexualized environment.

This is particularly the case for girls who may behave as pubertal adolescents, adopting a highly sexualized presentation of self that is promoted by a narcissistic culture so that they position themselves as objects to be admired, which may complicate their later experience of love and desire (Kernberg, 1998; González-Torres, personal communication, 2022).

Research studies have affirmed Kernberg's view of continuity between a narcissistic culture and narcissistic traits in the individual. That almost 10% of young people aged 20–29 meet criteria for narcissistic pathology (Stinson et al., 2008) and 25% of college students show marked narcissistic traits (Twenge et al., 2008) speaks to the point that the characteristic pathologies of our age represent amplifications of the underlying character structure. Twenge and Campbell and their colleagues have documented a systematic rise in narcissistic traits among college students over the past three decades (Foster et al., 2003; Twenge et al., 2008), evident in self-promoting behaviors, unrealistically inflated self-esteem, entitled expectations about careers, and indifference to the welfare of others observed in the so-called "Me Generation". A social context of increasing affluence, income inequality, and social and educational privilege has led, in their view, to a "narcissism epidemic" (see Donnellan et al., 2009, for a dissenting view). In a recent meta-analysis of 85 samples of American college students (encompassing studies done between 1979 and 2006), Twenge and colleagues (2008) found that college students have scored progressively higher on narcissistic traits (as measured by the NPI, a self-report measure that measures adaptive as well as maladaptive aspects of narcissism) from the early 1980s to 2006. In the early 1980s, average college students scored at the 50th percentile of NPI scores. In 2006, average college students scored in the 65th percentile of NPI scores. The authors also found that the mean NPI score of college students in 2006 was comparable to that of a sample of film stars, reality TV stars, and musicians (Young & Pinsky, 2006; Twenge et al., 2008). While high scores on the NPI do not necessarily translate into NPD or PN, the NPI does measure narcissistic traits that may be characteristic of subclinical levels of NPD that are continuous with the disorder (Cain et al., 2008; Paris, 2014). Indeed, other epidemiological studies have confirmed this trend towards increases in NPD and PN in both the clinical and general population. In the survey of a nationally representative sample of over 35,000 Americans conducted by Stinson et al. (2008), 9.5% of individuals in their twenties reported symptoms of NPD, compared with only

3.2% of respondents over age 65 or the overall rate of 6.2% of the general population. But in a reanalysis of the dataset that used more stringent criteria for NPD diagnosis, Trull and colleagues (2010) also found higher rates of NPD among younger participants, even though there was a decline in overall prevalence rates of NPD (1.2% for females; 0.7% for males). Even the latter rates make NPD a "highly prevalent disorder" in the view of Paris (2014), who has surmised that "if, as Twenge has suggested, trait narcissism is increasing, the prevalence of diagnosable NPD could also be increasing" (p. 221).

Thus, as Kernberg and, Lasch have predicted, the rise in narcissistic traits and NPD appears to be the consequence of a convergence of social and historical forces in contemporary society, but the extent to which this leads to more severe forms of narcissistic pathology is a complex process. Social and psychological perspectives on narcissism are mutually interpenetrating, although ultimately distinct and irreducible. Society reaches into the individual to shape them in its own image and for its own requirements, but within the individual, social processes are transformed into intrapsychic structures, governed by their own language and laws (Adorno, 1967, 1968; Adorno & Horkheimer, 1944/1972). The tools of social theory can help us to understand how society constitutes the individual, producing social character types, but it is the tools of psychoanalysis that enable us to decode the highly variable ways, pathological as well as nonpathological, in which social sedimentation settles within the individual psyche.

Malignant Narcissism in Large and Small Groups

Recently, Kernberg's investigations of the relationship between narcissistic pathology in individuals and social pathology in groups have focused on the historical circumstances in which there can be large group regression to malignant narcissistic mechanisms in the face of economic insecurity and cultural or political crises that threaten the identity or even survival of the group. While, under ordinary circumstances, the tension or distinction between individual and collective or group narcissism may be maintained so that narcissistic traits in the general populace do not necessarily foster dramatic increases in narcissistic pathology, under situations of group regression, narcissistic leaders may emerge who foster regression to primitive forms of narcissism in the citizenry. This may lead to an upsurge of primitive defenses of splitting into good and bad factions, demonization of and even savagery towards out-groups on whom are projected all that is unacceptable or deplorable, and a rapid reorganization of the dominant ideology to justify such behaviors and ideas. In formulating his theory of the large group regression and malignant narcissism, Kernberg has synthesized the psychoanalytic work of Freud on *Group Psychology and the Analysis of the Ego* (1921/1955) and of Bion (1961) on the basic assumption in small groups, as well as synthesized his own work on sanctioned social violence in times of political crisis with the work of political theorists such as Turquet (1975) on regression in large groups, Canetti (1984) on massification, and Snyder (2017) on the demise of democracy and the rise of tyranny. Drawing on the work of these theorists, Kernberg (2020) has further developed the basic principle of massification, or the process by which there are alterations in individual psyche and social behavior that occur when the individual becomes swept into a large group process, particularly in times of political upheaval or social transition. In certain historical circumstances, including war, trauma, economic crisis, and/or extreme political polarization, and under the sway of leaders with significant narcissistic and/or paranoid tendencies, such alterations may develop quite rapidly, sometimes independent of individual personality organization in normal individuals, or sometimes mobilizing individual pathology to serve the needs and interests of the larger group.

In small groups, described by Bion (1961) as "basic assumption groups", such regressions can take three different forms. In the first, the dependency group, members band together and compete for love and nurturance from an idealized leader, who is seen as omnipotent and omniscient. Should such dependency needs be frustrated, the group will seek out a more overtly grandiose narcissistic leader who devalues the members, even treating them as dependent and inferior. In the second small group, the fight flight group, there is a tendency to seek out a leader with paranoid as well as narcissistic traits who accepts the division into positive and negative, good and bad actors and sectors of experience, leading the group in their attacks on the bad out-group. Finally, in the third group, the pairing group, there is idealization of an admired couple or pair that embodies love and eroticism, inspiring group members to privilege sexual intimacy. Such a group designates a leader who is mature and wise, and protective of the privacy and intimacy of the sexual life of the couple. The oedipal strivings of the group function to protect group members against regression to dependent and/or fight-flight group mechanisms characterized by primitive defenses of splitting between in- and out-groups, primitive idealization, and projective identification of aggression and/or regression to preoedipal or latency age functioning, as described earlier. The unstructured nature of small groups may lead to regression to such basic assumption groups when there is a breakdown of task functions and the structure of the group. Narcissistic (grandiose and idealizing) defenses and mechanisms are operative, to some extent, in such regressions.

Under socially traumatic conditions, that is, in times of political, economic, or cultural strife when the group's identity or survival is at stake, individuals may be swept into mass movements where regressive mechanisms may take a more drastic form. In such situations, with the loss of a sense of identity and role differentiation or role status, there may be rapidly escalating anxiety, fear and aggression, and a loss of a sense of individual will, agency, and efficacy. Under such circumstances, when group and individual identities are challenged, individuals may forge a new social identity through mutual identifications with members of a subgroup, which may function as a "second skin" (Kernberg, 2020). The end result may be a shedding of or recalibration in individual and group identity. Allegiance to a leader with malignant narcissism may restore a sense of identity cohesion by bolstering the subgroup's mutual identifications with each other and by promising the restoration of a tribal form of supremacy, often at the expense of demonized outgroups who may be subject to persecution and even annihilation. Humanistic ideals of individual autonomy, social responsibility, and equality, are subsumed in the group identity and group imperatives.

Kernberg's theory of malignant narcissism in leaders provides a vehicle for understanding the convergence between socially sanctioned violence and social trends towards narcissism. Specifically, Kernberg (2003) sees a continuum between malignant narcissism in demagogic leaders and the extreme paranoid and narcissistic ideologies that characterize totalitarian regimes. In such regimes, the total control of the media, armed forces, and social and economic life submerges individual will and conscience, leading to socially sanctioned regression to violent behavior and even collusion with genocide in the general citizenry, many of whose members do not necessarily have severe narcissistic pathology. In the normative population, the immaturity and rigidity of internalized object relations with concomitant deficiencies in ego and superego functions may render the individual prone to narcissistic injuries in the face of disappointment in entitled or grandiose expectations engendered by social or economic crises or disappointments. The latter, in turn, may foster or amplify narcissistic traits that predispose the individual to embrace regressive ideologies put forth by narcissistic leaders who promise the restoration of supremacy, power, and glory at the group level, redressing the traumatic past through persecution of outgroups, and inviting participation in an imagined future that amplifies and mythologizes past glories (Kernberg, 1989).

Particularly problematic are leaders who embody a combination of paranoid traits, ego syntonic aggression, sadism, and antisocial behaviors such as lying, cheating, and humiliating or bullying others. Such leaders with malignant narcissism may function at a high level as long as their primitive defenses of projection and splitting stabilize and empower the self and consolidate the group identity. They may spearhead mass movements that unleash rationalized hatred and destructiveness in ordinary individuals. In such situations, one sees the resuscitation and unleashing of primitive object relations infused with aggression, the potential for which resides within each individual, usually tempered and transmuted into normal, tolerable negative feelings or ambivalence through ordinary familial and social interactions. In totalitarian regimes, aggression in the citizenry may be channelled into atavistic strivings for idealization of self and country (particularly in situations of unresolved historical trauma, economic deprivation, or diminution of status on the world stage), leading, in extreme cases, to sanctioned social violence towards out-groups. As Kernberg (2003a) puts it, "the dimensions of narcissistic and paranoid regression thus emerge as major axes around which regressive social pathology crystallizes, and they link the psychopathology of the leader with the nature of regression in small and large unstructured groups" (p. 8). There are a number of mediating factors, then, between individual narcissistic pathology and a social order organized along paranoid and narcissistic lines, with the main one being the personality structure of the leader and its interdigitation with the personality structure of their followers. "The self-assuredness of the leader and the expansion of his paranoid, grandiose and aggressive behavior go hand in hand with the increase of a sense of power, freedom, volent behavior, and triumphant excitement of the regressed large group" (Kernberg, 2020, p. 8). Kernberg observes that individuals with grandiose narcissistic traits or pathology are most likely to be swept up into and assume leadership roles in such a mass movement, forming an impenetrable social block. In such a regressive group, the leader embodies the ego ideal of the individual and the group, collapsing the distinction between the two, while there is also a projection of superego and moral systems onto the leader. Consequently, the individual surrenders their judgment, will, and agency to the leader, fostering a sense of self-righteousness and freedom from guilt in the face of aggression towards out-groups, which empowers and binds group members' identification to each other. The slavish submission to irrational authority and collusion with forms of rationalized aggression and hatred that Kernberg observes in the general nonclinical population in situations of large group regression all have their counterparts in the clinical picture of the syndrome of malignant narcissism developed by Kernberg. By contrast, those individuals who might under ordinary circumstances become effective and benign leaders, that is, those who are intelligent, thoughtful, reflective, and observing with a well-developed moral compass that is respectful of, but not slavishly adherent to, group norms: a well-regulated, healthy narcissism that allows for maintenance of a sense of value and direction regardless of external vicissitudes; and a well-integrated world of internalized object relations, may be marginalized, relegated to the status of outsiders, social pariahs, or worse.

While these contributions on narcissism as a social and clinical phenomenon invite us to consider narcissism and its disorders from a wider angle, they nevertheless maintain distinctions between the social and the psychological, albeit considering conditions in which these two spheres may collapse. Character development always results from an adaptation between culturally fostered patterns of self and identity formation, on the one hand, and the imperatives of the intrapsychic world of drive, affect, and object relations, on the other. From a psychoanalytic object relations perspective, one sphere cannot be reduced to the other.

From the object relations point of view, in the normative situation, infantile narcissistic strivings may coexist with rudimentary forms of relatedness and dependency, and both will undergo transformations to more mature forms of self-definition and relatedness in the course of development. By contrast, in cases of individuals with PN and NPD, the activation and persistence of infantile narcissism predisposes the individual towards ready assimilation to and overvaluation of a narcissistic culture.

The Contributions of Contemporary Object Relations Theory to Understanding the Links between Individual and Collective Narcissism

There are several aspects of object relations theory that work to miti-
gate against a direct correspondence between social structure and individual personality disorders. First, Kernberg (1993) integrates his
conceptualizations of narcissism and its disorders with drive theory,
stipulating that libido and aggression are bound up in a complex mesh
of affectively charged early experiences with objects from birth on.
In his view, "[t]he development of normal and pathological narcissism always involves the relationship of self-representation to object
representation and external objects as well as instinctual conflicts
involving both libido and aggression" (Kernberg, 1984, p. 189). By
maintaining the tension between drives and object relations and by
emphasizing the significance of eroticism and sexuality for both narcissism and love relations, Kernberg (1994) preserves erotic love as a
potential sphere of deep and intense intimacy, mutuality, privacy, and
creative self-expression for the couple that renders them potentially
resistant to group norms and mores, and particularly "the efforts of
masses to achieve uniform, multiple identifications with each other
and with their leader" (p. 89). A case in point is Orwell's (1950) depic-
tion in *1984* of how erotic love shared by one couple must be destroyed
because it challenges the enforced uniformity, conformity, and anti-
libidinal attitudes imposed by the totalitarian regime of Big Brother. In
this regime, sexuality is denuded of eroticism and yoked to the needs
of the state for reproduction to produce more workers. This is because
erotic desire threatens the mobilization of massive primitive aggression at the group level, epitomized by the required daily "Two Minutes
Hate" (Orwell, 1950, p. 9), a daily ritual in which there is an orgiastic
outpouring of vituperation against enemies and out-groups (see also
Gonzalez-Torres & Frenandez-Rivas, 2015, for a discussion of *1984*).

> The horrible thing about the Two Minute Hate was not that one was
> obliged to act a part, but that it was impossible to avoid joining in…
> within 30 seconds the pretense was always unnecessary. A hide-
> ous ecstasy of fear and vindictiveness, a desire to kill, to torture…
> seemed to flow through the whole group like an electric current…
>
> (Orwell, 1950, p. 9)

In such situations, erotic desire is subsumed and even extinguished by primitive aggression at the group level, rather than subsuming aggression which may enrich eroticism when it is contained within the couple.

Kernberg conceptualizes love relations and object relations, in general, as a complex admixture of love and aggression and narcissistic and object-oriented strivings and identifications, in contrast to other theorists who posit a radical disjunction between object relations of the narcissistic and object-related types or see aggression as a by-product or "breakdown product" of frustrated narcissistic needs (Kohut, 1971). Kernberg points out that in intimate relationships the object is always loved for both its unique otherness *and* its capacity to enhance the self, such that "the investment of objects and the investment of the self in the gratifying relations with such objects go hand in hand" (Kernberg, 1975, p. 323). Kernberg stipulates that no single developmental line can be supraordinated to others in understanding normal and pathological development. Instead, object love and narcissism in his view evolve out of a shared developmental matrix, and both are fueled by intense affective experiences of love and hate, pleasure and frustration, that organize the drives of eroticism (libido) and aggression. Thus, the drives in his view, although rooted in early affective experiences and exchanges with caregivers, are themselves constructed in part along the inborn affective axes of love and hate and cannot be eradicated as primary motivational systems. Indeed, it is the primacy and autonomy of such motivational systems based on inborn affect systems that provide the locus of resistance to collective narcissism in the social sphere and to the seduction of authoritarianism.

From an object relations point of view, the origins of the self are inherently social in that they grow out of an inborn proclivity towards reciprocal interactions and mutual affective exchanges from birth on, evident in the inborn capacity to "share codes for perception and action" (Ammaniti & Gallese, 2008, p. 141). In numerous studies that are beyond the scope of this work, developmental researchers have now shown that infants from birth on are adept in responding to their caregivers, in engaging them in social interactions which they internalize in increasingly complex ways. Indeed, these inborn codes, as well as rudimentary capacities for internalization of them, are evident in the infant's capacity to imitate the motor actions and gestures of others (Legerstee, 2005), to recognize and reproduce a caregiver's facial expressions, and to show primitive empathy or affective resonance with the states of others (e.g., infants cry in response to the cry of other infants, although this may vary according to infant temperament (Singer & Hein, 2012)). Infants in normative development also show differentiated patterns of response to different individuals, preferring attachment figures over other conspecifics, and engaging in contingent, synchronous interactions with them that are observable as early as four months in highly idiosyncratic dyadic patterns of mutual regulation and response (Tronick, 1998, 2007; Ammaniti & Gallese, 2008). The foregoing aspects of infant self- and interpersonal functioning are internalized in increasingly complex sets of integrated and differentiated mental representations, which may have their origins in the infant's experience of actual parent-child transactions, but these representations of interactions come to constitute a discrete and separate sphere of intrapsychic reality (Ammanitti & Gallese, 2008; Kernberg, 2015). In the view of contemporary object relations theorists, sexuality, fantasy, impulse, and drive enrich and expand the arc of the representational world, creating from the beginning areas of tension between the psychological and the social, the individual and society that cannot be totally eradicated.

In the normative situation, infantile narcissistic strivings coexist with rudimentary forms of relatedness and dependency, and both, in the course of optimal development, will undergo transformations to more mature forms of self-definition and object love. By contrast, in individuals with narcissistic pathology, there is investment in a pathological self-structure, the pathological grandiose self, which has been associated with insecure attachment and deficits in mentalization, both signs of disturbances in object-relating that may predispose individuals to overvalue and assimilate to the imperatives of a narcissistic culture.

The recent formulations by Kernberg illustrate that the understanding of narcissism, normal and pathological, varies with shifts in historical and social conditions. The culture of consumption, the breakdown of extended family structures, the shifting views of gender and sexuality, the increase in income inequality, the rise of religious fundamentalism, the rapid development of artificial intelligence, and the hegemony of social media as a vehicle for self-definition and self-aggrandizement have led to new cultural experiences of the self. These social trends have reconfigured the dialogue about the relationship between social and psychological aspects of narcissism, and about the nature of narcissistic pathology itself. The identification of more covert or vulnerable forms of narcissistic pathology, as delineated earlier, has changed our understanding of the content and the form of narcissistic disorders. Changes in sociohistorical conditions thus will demand ongoing reformulations of the nature of narcissistic pathology, as well as of the relationship between social narcissism and NPD as a particular pathological structuring of the personality.

References

Adorno, T. (1967). Sociology and psychology (part I). *New Left Review, 46*(1), 90.

Adorno, T. (1968). Sociology and psychology (part II). *New Left Review, 47*(1), 79–97.

Adorno, T.W., Frenkel-Brunswik, E., Levinson, D.J., & Sanford, N. (1950). *The authoritarian personality*. Harper & Brothers.

Adorno, T.W., & Horkheimer, M. (1972). *Dialectic of enlightenment* (J. Cumming, Trans.). Herder and Herder. (Original work published 1944).

Afifi, T.O., Mather, A., Boman, J., Fleisher, W., Enns, M.W., MacMillan, H., & Sareen, J. (2011). Childhood adversity and personality disorders: Results from a nationally representative population-based study. *Journal of Psychiatric Research, 45*(6), 814–822. https://doi.org/10.1016/j.jpsychires.2010.11.008.

American Psychiatric Association (1980). Diagnostic and statistical manual of mental disorders (3rd ed.).

American Psychiatric Association (2013). Diagnostic and statistical manual of mental disorders (5th ed.). https://doi.org/10.1176/appi.books.9780890425596.

Ammaniti, M., & Gallese, V. (2014). *The birth of intersubjectivity: Psychodynamics, neurobiology, and the self*. W.W. Norton & Company, Inc.

Appelbaum, A. (2006). Supportive psychoanalytic psychotherapy for borderline patients: An empirical approach. *American Journal of Psychoanalysis, 66*(4), 317–332. https://doi.org/10.1007/s11231-006-9026-2.

Applebaum, A. (2020). *Twilight of democracy: The seductive lure of authoritarianism*. Anchor Books.

Auchincloss, E.L., & Samberg, E. (Eds.) (2012). *Psychoanalytic terms and concepts*. Yale University Press.

Bataille, G. (1986). *Erotism: Death and sensuality*. City Lights Books.

Bernstein, J., Zimmerman, M., & Auchincloss, E.L. (2015). Transference-focused psychotherapy during residency training: An aide to learning psychodynamic psychotherapy. *Psychodynamic Psychiatry, 43*(2), 201–222. https://doi.org/10.1521/pdps.2015.43.2.201.

Biberdzic, M., Normandin, L., Weiner, A., Ensink, & Clarkin, J.F. (2023). *LPODq (Levels of Personality Organization and Development questionnaire)*. Unpublished manuscript.

Bion, W.R. (1961). *Experiences in groups and other papers*. Tavistock/ Routledge.

Blatt, S.J., D'Afflitti, J.P., & Quinlan, D.M. (1976). Experiences of depression in normal young adults. *Journal of Abnormal psychology, 85*(4), 383–389. https://doi.org/10.1037//0021-843x.85.4.383.

Bowlby, J. (1980). *Attachment and loss: Volume 3: Loss: Sadness and depression*. Basic Books.

Britton, R. (1992). The Oedipus situation and the depressive position. In R. Anderson (Ed.), *Clinical lectures on Klein and Bion* (pp. 34–45). Tavistock/Routledge.

Britton, R. (2004). Subjectivity, objectivity, and triangular space. *The Psychoanalytic Quarterly, 73*(1), 47–61. https://doi.org/10.1002/j.2167-4086.2004. tb00152.x.

Buchheim, A., & Diamond, D. (2018). Attachment and borderline personality disorder. *Psychiatric Clinics, 41*(4), 651–668. https://doi.org/10.1016/j. psc.2018.07.010.

Cain, N.M., Pincus, A.L., & Ansell, E.B. (2008). Narcissism at the crossroads: Phenotypic description of pathological narcissism across clinical theory, social/personality psychology, and psychiatric diagnosis. *Clinical Psychology Review, 28*(4), 638–656. http://doi.org/10.1016/j.cpr.2007.09.006.

Caligor, E., Kernberg, O.F., Clarkin, J.F., & Yeomans, F.E. (2018). *Psychodynamic therapy for personality pathology: Treating self and interpersonal functioning*. American Psychiatric Association Publishing.

Campbell, W.K., & Campbell, S.M. (2009). On the self-regulatory dynamics created by the particular benefits and costs of narcissism: A contextual reinforcement model and examination of leadership. *Self Identity, 8*(2–3), 214–232. https://doi.org/10.1080/15298860802505129.

Canetti, E. (1984). *Crowds and power* (C. Stewart, Trans.). Farrar, Straus, and Giroux. (Original work published 1960).

Carlson, E.B., Smith, S.R., Palmieri, P.A., Dalenberg, C., Ruzek, J.I., Kimerling, R., Burling, T.A., & Spain, D.A. (2011). Development and validation of a brief self-report measure of trauma exposure: The Trauma History Screen. *Psychological Assessment, 23*(2), 463–477. https://doi.org/10.1037/ a0022294.

Carrasco, B. (2013). An empirical analysis of adult romantic attachment and sexuality. *Dissertation Abstracts International: Section B: The Sciences and Engineering, 74*(3-B(E)).

Carsky, M. (2013). Supportive psychoanalytic therapy for personality disorders. *Psychotherapy, 50*(3), 443–448. https://doi.org/10.1037/a0032156.

Cater, T.E., Zeigler-Hill, V., & Vonk, J. (2011). Narcissism and recollections of early life experiences. *Personality and Individual Differences, 51*(8), 935–939. https://doi.org/10.1016/j.paid.2011.07.023.

Clarkin, J.F., Caligor, E., & Sowislo, J. (2021). TFP Extended: Development and recent advances. *Psychodynamic Psychiatry, 49*(2), 188–214. https:// doi.org/10.1521/pdps.2021.49.2.188.

Clarkin, J.F., Caligor, E., Stern, B.L., & Kernberg, O.F. (2004). *Structured Interview of Personality Organization (STIPO)*. Unpublished manuscript. Personality Disorders Institute, Weill Medical College of Cornell University.

Clarkin, J.F., Caligor, E., Stern, B.L., & Kernberg, O.F. (2017). *Structured Interview for Personality Organization – Revised (STIPO-R)*. Unpublished manuscript. Personality Disorders Institute, Weill Cornell Medical College of Cornell University.

Clarkin, J.F., Foelsch, P.A., Levy, K.N., Hull, J.W., Delaney, J.C., & Kernberg, O.F. (2001). The development of a psychodynamic treatment for patients with borderline personality disorder: A preliminary study of behavioral change. *Journal of Personality Disorders, 15*(6), 487–495. https://doi.org/10.1521/pedi.15.6.487.19190.

Clarkin, J.F., Levy, K.N., Lenzenweger, M.F., & Kernberg, O.F. (2007). Evaluating three treatments for borderline personality disorder: A multiwave study. *American Journal of Psychiatry, 164*(6), 922–928. https://doi.org/10.1176/ajp.2007.164.6.922.

Clarkin, J.F., Meehan, K.B., DePanfilis, C., & Doering, S. (2023). Empirical developments in transference-focused psychotherapy. *American Journal of Psychotherapy, 76*(1), 39–45. https://doi.org/10.1176/appi.psychotherapy.20220017.

Clarkin, J.F., Yeomans, F.E., & Kernberg, O.F. (1999). *Psychotherapy for borderline personality.* John Wiley & Sons, Inc.

Clarkin, J.F., Yeomans, F.E., & Kernberg, O.F. (2006). *Psychotherapy for borderline personality: Focusing on object relations* (2nd ed.). American Psychiatric Publishing.

Cohen, L.J., Foster, M., Nesci, C., Tanis, T., Halmi, W., & Galynker, I. (2012). How do different types of childhood maltreatment relate to adult personality pathology? *The Journal of Nervous and Mental Disease, 201*(3), 234–43. https://doi.org/10.1097/NMD.0b013e3182848ac4.

Crawford, M.J., Koldobsky, N., Mulder, R., & Tyrer, P. (2011). Classifying personality disorder according to severity. *Journal of Personality Disorders, 25*(3), 321–330. https://doi.org/10.1521/pedi.2011.25.3.321.

Cuevas, P., Camacho, J., Mejia, R., Rosario, I., Parres, R., Mendoza, J., & Lopez, D. (2000). Cambios en la psicopatologia del trastorno limitrofe de la personalidad, en los pacientes trtados con la psicoterapia psicodinamica. *Salud Mental, 23*(6), 1–11.

Czarna, A.Z., Dufner, M., & Clifton, A.D. (2014). The effects of vulnerable and grandiose narcissism on liking-based and disliking-based centrality in social networks. *Journal of Research in Personality, 50*, 42–45. https://doi.org/10.1016/j.jrp.2014.02.004.

Dalewijk, H.J., & van Luyn, B. (2005). The Symfora tapes: Master clinicians at work [DVD]. Symfora Groep, Centers for Mental Health.

Delaney, J.C., & Yeomans, F.E. (2021). Functions of the treatment contract in TFP. *Psychodynamic Psychiatry, 49*(2), 322–338. https://doi.org/10.1521/pdps.2021.49.2.322.

DePanfilis, C., Schito, G., Generali, I, Gozzi, L.A., Ossola, P., Marchesi, C., & Grecucci, A. (2019). Emotions at the border: Increased punishment behavior during fair interpersonal exchanges in borderline personality disorder. *Journal of Abnormal Psychology, 128*(2), 162–172. https://doi.org/10.1037/abn0000404.

Diamond, D., Clarkin, J., Levine, H., Levy, K.N., Foelsch, P., & Yeomans, F.E. (1999). Borderline conditions and attachment: A preliminary report. *Psychoanalytic Inquiry, 19*(5), 831–884. https://doi.org/10.1080/07351699909534278.

Diamond, D., Clarkin, J.F., Levy, K.N., Meehan, K.B., Cain, N.M., Yeomans, F.E., & Kernberg, O.F. (2014a). Change in attachment and reflective function in borderline patients with and without comorbid narcissistic personality disorder in transference focused psychotherapy. *Contemporary Psychoanalysis, 50*(1–2), 175–210. https://doi.org/10.1080/00107530.2014.880316.

Diamond, D., Keefe, J.R., Hörz-Sagstetter, S., Fischer-Kern, M., Doering, S., & Buchheim, A. (2023). Changes in attachment representation and personality organization in transference-focused psychotherapy. *American Journal of Psychotherapy, 76*(1), 31–38. https://doi.org/10.1176/appi.psychotherapy.20220018.

Diamond, D., Levy, K.N., Clarkin, J.F., Fischer-Kern, M., Cain, N.M., Doering, S., Hörz, S., & Buchheim, A. (2014b). Attachment and mentalization in female patients with comorbid narcissistic and borderline personality disorder. *Personality Disorders: Theory, Research, and Treatment, 5*(4), 428–433. https://doi.org/10.1037/per0000065.

Diamond, D., Stovall-McClough, C., Clarkin, J.F., & Levy, K.N. (2003). Patient-therapist attachment in the treatment of borderline personality disorder. *Bulletin of the Menninger Clinic, 67*(3), 227–259. https://doi.org/10.1521/bumc.67.3.227.23433.

Diamond, D., & Yeomans, F.E. (2007). Oedipal love and conflict in the transference-countertransference matrix: Its impact on attachment security and mentalization. In D. Diamond, S. Blatt, & J. Litchenberg (Eds.), *Attachment & sexuality* (pp. 201–236). The Analytic Press (Taylor & Francis).

Diamond, D., Yeomans, F.E., Stern, B.L, & Kernberg, O.F. (2022). *Treating pathological narcissism with transference-focused psychotherapy.* The Guilford Press.

Diamond, D., Yeomans, F.E., Stern, B., Levy, K.N., Hörz, S., Doering, S., Fischer-Kern, M., Delaney, J., & Clarkin, J.F. (2013). Transference focused psychotherapy for patients with comorbid narcissistic and borderline personality disorder. *Psychoanalytic Inquiry, 33*(6), 527–551. https://doi.org/10.1080/07351690.2013.815087.

Doering, S., Hörz, S., Rentrop, M., Fischer-Kern, M., Schuster, P., Benecke, C., Buchheim, A., Martius, P., & Buchheim, P. (2010). Transference-focused psychotherapy v. treatment by community psychotherapists for borderline personality disorder: Randomised controlled trial. *The British Journal of Psychiatry: The Journal of Mental Science, 196*(5), 389–395. https://doi.org/10.1192/bjp.bp.109.070177.

Donegan, N.H., Sanislow, C.A., Blumberg, H.P., Fulbright, R.K., Lacadie, C., Skudlarski, P., Gore, J.C., Olson, I.R., McGlashan, T.H., & Wexler, B.E. (2003). Amygdala hyperreactivity in borderline personality disorder: Implications for emotional dysregulation. *Biological Psychiatry, 54*(11), 1284–1293. https://doi.org/10.1016/s0006-3223(03)00636-x.

Donnellan, M.B., Trzesniewski, K.H., & Robins, R.W. (2009). An emerging epidemic of narcissism or much ado about nothing? *Journal of Research in Personality, 43*(3), 498–501. https://doi.org/10.1016/j.jrp.2008.12.010.

Edershile, E.A., & Wright, A.G. (2022). Narcissism dynamics. *Social and Personality Psychology Compass, 16*(1), Article e12649. https://doi.org/10.1111/spc3.12649.

Ensink, K., Chretien, S., Normandin, L., Begin, M., Daigle, D., & Fonagy, P. (2017). Pathological narcissism in adolescents: Relationships with childhood maltreatment and internalizing and externalizing difficulties. *Adolescent Psychiatry, 7*(4), 300–314. https://doi.org/10.2174/2210676608666180119165731.

Erikson, E.H. (1950). *Identity and the life cycle.* International Universities Press.

Erikson, E.H. (1956). The problem of ego identity. *Journal of the American Psychoanalytic Association, 4*, 56–121. https://doi.org/10.1177/000306515600400104.

Fairbairn, W.R.D. (1952). *Psychoanalytic studies of the personality.* Routledge.

Fairbairn, W.R.D. (1954). *An object relations theory of the personality.* Basic Books.

Fertuck, E.A., Grinband, J., & Stanley, B. (2013). Facial trust appraisal negatively biased in borderline personality disorder. *Psychiatry Research, 207*(3), 195–202. https://doi.org/10.1016/j.psychres.2013.01.004.

First, M.B., & Gibbon, M. (2004). The structured clinical interview for DSM-IV axis I disorders (SCID-I) and the structured clinical interview for DSM-IV axis II disorders (SCID-II). In M.J. Hilsenroth, & D.L. Segal (Eds.), *Comprehensive handbook of psychological assessment, Vol. 2. Personality assessment* (pp. 134–143). John Wiley & Sons, Inc.

Fonagy, P., Gergely, G., Jurist, E., & Target, M. (2002). *Affect regulation, mentalization, and the development of the self.* Other Press.

Fonagy, P., Steele, H., & Steele, M. (1991). Maternal representations of attachment during pregnancy predict the organization of infant-mother attachment at one year of age. *Child Development, 62*(5), 891–905. https://doi.org/10.1111/j.1467-8624.1991.tb01578.x.

Fonagy, P., & Target, M. (1997). Attachment and reflective function: Their role in self-organization. *Development and Psychopathology, 9*(4), 679–700. https://doi.org/10.1017/s0954579497001399.

Foster, J.D., Campbell, W.K., & Twenge, J.M. (2003). Individual differences in narcissism: Inflated self-views across the lifespan and around the world. *Journal of Research in Personality, 37*(6), 469–486. https://doi.org/10.1016/S0092-6566(03)00026-6.

Freud, S. (1921/1955). Group psychology and the analysis of the ego. In J. Strachey (Ed., Trans.), *The standard edition of the complete psychological works of Sigmund Freud* (Vol. 18, pp. 65–144). MacMillan.

Freud, S. (1957). On narcissism: An introduction. In J. Strachey (Ed., Trans.), *The standard edition of the complete psychological works of Sigmund Freud* (Vol. 14, pp. 73–102). Hogarth Press. (Original work published 1914).

Freud, S. (1961). The ego and the id. In J. Strachey (Ed., Trans.), *The standard edition of the complete psychological works of Sigmund Freud* (Vol. 19, pp. 19–27). Hogarth Press. (Original work published 1923).

Freud, S. (1964). An outline of psycho-analysis. In J. Strachey (Ed., Trans.), *The standard edition of the complete psychological works of Sigmund Freud* (Vol. 23, pp. 144–205). MacMillan. (Original work published 1940).

George, C., Kaplan, N., & Main, M. (1985). *The adult attachment interview.* Unpublished manuscript. University of California at Berkeley.

Gonzalez-Torres, M.A., & Fernandez-Rivas, A. (2015). Female sexuality, nationalism, and large group identity. *The American Journal of Psychoanalysis, 75*(4), 416–437. https://doi.org/10.1057/ajp.2015.47.

Gunderson, J. (2017, November 8). *Treatments for borderline personality disorder* [Grand rounds lecture]. Weill Cornell Medical College Psychiatry Grand Rounds, New York.

Gunderson, J., & Links, P.S. (2014). *Handbook of good psychiatric management for borderline personality disorder.* American Psychiatric Publishing.

Gunderson, J., Frank, A.F., Ronningstam, E.F., Wachter, S. Lynch, V.J., & Wolf, P.J. (1989). Early discontinuance of borderline patients from psychotherapy. *Journal of Nervous and Mental Disease, 177*(1), 38–42. https://doi.org/10.1097/00005053-198901000-00006.

Gunderson, J., Ronningstam, E., & Smith, L. (1996). Narcissistic personality disorder. In T.A. Widiger, A.J. Frances, H.A. Pincus, R. Ross, M.B. First, & W.W. David (Eds.), *DSM-IV sourcebook* (Vol. 2, pp. 745–746). American Psychiatric Association.

Gunderson, J., & Ronningstam, E. (2001). Differentiating narcissistic and antisocial personality disorders. *Journal of Personality Disorders, 15*(2), 103–109.

Hersh, R.G., Caligor, E., & Yeomans, F.E. (2016). *Fundamentals of transference-focused psychotherapy: Applications in psychiatric and general medical settings.* Springer.

Hesse, E., & Main, M. (2006). Frightened, threatening, and dissociative parental behavior in low-risk samples: Description, discussion, and interpretations. *Development and Psychopathology, 18*(2), 309–343. https://doi.org/10.1017/S0954579406060172.

Hilsenroth, M.J., Holdwick, D.J., Jr., Castlebury, F.D., & Blais, M.A. (1998). The effects of DSM-IV cluster B personality disorder symptoms on the termination and continuation of psychotherapy. *Psychotherapy: Theory, Research, Practice, Training, 35*(2), 163–176. https://doi.org/10.1037/h0087845.

Hoglund, C.L. (1996). Narcissistic features, shame, anger and gender differences in adults exposed to emotionally abusive family environments (Publication No. 9638286) [Doctoral dissertation, University of Wyoming]. ProQuest Dissertations Publishing.

Høglend, P., Bøgwald, K.P., Amlo, S., Marble, A., Ulberg, R., Sjaastad, M.C., Sørbye, O., Heyerdahl, O., & Johansson, P. (2008). Transference interpretations in dynamic psychotherapy: Do they really yield sustained effects? *The American Journal of Psychiatry, 165*(6), 763–771. https://doi.org/10.1176/appi.ajp.2008.07061028.

Hopwood, C.J., Malone, J.C., Ansell, E.B., Sanislow, C.A., Grilo, C.M., McGlashan, T.H., Pinto, A., Markowitz, J.C., Shea, M.T., Skodol, A.E., Gunderson, J.G., Zanarini, M.C., & Morey, L.C. (2011). Personality assessment in DSM-5: Empirical support for rating severity, style, and traits. *Journal of Personality Disorders, 25*(3), 305–320.

Hörz, S., Clarkin, J.F., Stern, B.L., & Caligor, E. (2012). The Structured Interview of Personality Organization (STIPO): An instrument to assess severity and change of personality pathology. In R.A. Levy, J.S. Ablon, & H. Kächele (Eds.), *Handbook of evidence-based psychodynamic psychotherapy* (3rd ed., pp. 571–592). Humana Press – Springer.

Huprich, S.K., Nelson, S.M., Paggeot, A., Lengu, K., & Albright, J. (2017). Object relations predict borderline personality disorder symptoms beyond emotional dysregulation, negative affect, and impulsivity. *Personal Disorders, 8*(1), 46–53. https://doi.org/10.1037/per0000188.

Jacobson, E. (1964). *The self and the object world.* International Universities Press.

Johnson, J.G., Cohen, P., Smailes, E.M., Skodol, A.E., Brown, J., & Oldham, J.M. (2001). Childhood verbal abuse and risk for personality disorders during adolescence and early adulthood. *Comprehensive Psychiatry, 42*(1), 16–23. https://doi.org/10.1053/comp.2001.19755.

Joseph, B., (1985). Transference: The total situation. *International Journal of Psychoanalysis,* 66(4), 447–454.

Kaplan, L.J. (1991). *Female perversions: The temptations of Emma Bovary.* Doubleday.

Kernberg, O.F. (1959a). Diagnosis and treatment of hysteria. *Boletín del Hospital San Juan de Dios,* 6, 132–138.

Kernberg, O.F. (1959b). Neurotic depression. *Boletín del Hospital San Juan de Dios,* 6, 218–230.

Kernberg, O.F. (1959c). Anxiety neurosis. *Boletín del Hospital San Juan de Dios,* 6, 328–340.

Kernberg, O.F. (1965). Three methods of research on psychoanalytic treatment. *International Mental Health Research Newsletter,* 7, 11–13.

Kernberg, O.F. (1966). Structural derivatives of object relations. *International Journal of Psychoanalysis,* 47, 236–253.

Kernberg, O.F. (1967). Borderline personality organization. *Journal of the American Psychoanalytic Association, 15*(3), 641–685.

Kernberg, O.F. (1968). The treatment of patients with borderline personality organization. *The International Journal of Psycho-analysis, 49*(4), 600–619.

Kernberg, O.F. (1975a). *Borderline conditions and pathological narcissism.* Jason Aronson, Inc.

Kernberg, O.F. (1975b). Modern hospital milieu treatment of schizophrenia. In S. Arieti, & G. Chrzanowski (Eds.), *New dimensions in psychiatry: A world view* (pp. 202–220). John Wiley and Sons.

Kernberg, O.F. (1976). *Object-relations theory and clinical psychoanalysis.* Jason Aronson, Inc.

Kernberg, O.F. (1977). Boundaries and structures in love relations. *Journal of the American Psychoanalytic Association, 25*(1), 81–114.

Kernberg, O.F. (1980). *Internal world and external reality: Object relations theory applied.* Jason Aronson, Inc.

Kernberg, O.F. (1981). Structural interviewing. *Psychiatric Clinics of North America, 4*(1), 169–195.

Kernberg, O.F. (1984). *Severe personality disorders: Psychotherapeutic strategies.* Yale University Press.

Kernberg, O.F. (1986). Narcissistic personality disorder. *The Personality Disorders and Neuroses, 1,* 219–231.

Kernberg, O.F. (1989). The temptations of conventionality. *International Review of Psycho-Analysis, 16*(2), 191–205.

Kernberg, O.F. (1992). *Aggression in personality disorders and perversion.* Yale University Press.

Kernberg, O.F. (1993). Convergences and divergences in contemporary psychoanalytic technique. *The International Journal of Psycho-Analysis, 74*(4), 659–673.

Kernberg, O.F. (1994). The erotic in film and in mass psychology. *Bulletin of the Menninger Clinic, 58*(1), 88–108.

Kernberg, O.F. (1995). *Love relations: Normality and pathology.* Yale University Press.

Kernberg, O.F. (2003). Socially sanctioned violence: The large group as society. In H. Weinberg, & S. Schneider (Eds.), *The large group re-visited: The herd, primal horde, crowds, and masses* (pp. 125–149). Jessica Kingsley Publishers Ltd.

Kernberg, O.F. (2004a). *Contemporary controversies in psychoanalytic theory, technique and their applications.* Yale University Press.

Kernberg, O.F. (2004b). *Aggressivity, narcissism and self-destructiveness in the psychotherapeutic relationship: New developments in the psychopathology and psychotherapy of severe personality disorders.* Yale University Press.

Kernberg, O.F. (2006). Identity: Recent findings and clinical implications. *The Psychoanalytic Quarterly, 75*(4), 969–1004. https://doi.org/10.1002/j.2167-4086.2006.tb00065.x.

Kernberg, O.F. (2007). The almost untreatable narcissistic patient. *Journal of the American Psychoanalytic Association, 55*(2), 503–539. https://doi.org/1 0.1177/00030651070550020701.

Kernberg, O.F. (2011). Limitations to the capacity to love. *The International Journal of Psychoanalysis, 92*(6), 1501–1515. https://doi.org/10.1111/ j.1745-8315.2011.00456.x.

Kernberg, O.F. (2012). *The inseparable nature of love and aggression: Clinical and theoretical perspectives.* American Psychiatric Publishing, Inc.

Kernberg, O.F. (2015). Neurobiological correlates of object relations theory: The relationship between neurobiological and psychodynamic development. *International Forum of Psychoanalysis, 24*(1), 38–46.

Kernberg, O.F. (2018). *Treatment of severe personality disorders: Resolution of aggression and recovery of eroticism.* American Psychiatric Association Publishing.

Kernberg, O.F. (2020). Malignant narcissism and large group regression. *The Psychoanalytic Quarterly, 89*(1), 1–24. https://doi.org/10.1080/00332828.2 020.1685342.

Kernberg, O.F. (2021). Extensions of psychoanalytic technique: The mutual influences of standard psychoanalysis and transference-focused psychotherapy. *Psychodynamic Psychiatry, 49*(4), 506–531.https://doi.org/10.1521/ pdps.2021.49.4.506.

Kernberg, O.F. (2022). Some implications of new developments in neurobiology for psychoanalytic object relations theory. *Neuropsychoanalysis, 24*(1), 3–12. https://doi.org/10.1080/15294145.2021.1995609.

Kernberg, O.F. (2023). *Hatred, emptiness, and hope: Transference-focused psychotherapy in personality disorders.* American Psychiatric Association Publishing.

Kernberg, P.F. (1998). Sexuality in the analysis of adolescents: Its impact on the transference-countertransference. *The International Journal of Psycho-Analysis, 79*(2), 366–367.

Kernberg, O.F., & Caligor, E. (2005). A psychoanalytic theory of personality disorders. In J.F. Clarkin, & M.F. Lenzenweger (Eds.), *Major theories of personality disorder* (2nd ed., pp. 115–156). The Guilford Press.

Kernberg, O.F., Selzer, M.A., Koenigsberg, H.W., Carr, A.C., & Appelbaum, A.H. (1989). *Psychodynamic psychotherapy of borderline patients.* Basic Books.

Kivity, Y., Levy, K.N., Kelly, K.M., & Clarkin, J.F. (2021). In session reflective functioning in psychotherapies for borderline personality disorder: The emotion regulatory role of reflective functioning. *Journal of Consulting and Clinical Psychology, 89*(9), 751–761. https://doi.org/10.1037/ccp0000674.

Klein, M. (1946). Notes on some schizoid mechanisms. *The International Journal of Psychoanalysis, 27*, 99–110.

Klein, M. (1957). *Envy and gratitude; a study of unconscious sources.* Basic Books.

Klein, M. (1975). A contribution to the psychogenesis of manic-depressive states (1935). In R. Money-Kyrle (Ed.), *Love, guilt and reparation and other works, 1921-1945* (1st ed., pp. 262–289). Hogarth Press.

Knight, R.P. (1953). Borderline states. *Bulletin of the Menninger Clinic, 17*, 1–12.

Kohut, H. (1971). *The analysis of the self: A systematic approach to the psychoanalytic treatment of narcissistic personality disorders.* University of Chicago Press.

Laplanche, J. (1997). The theory of seduction and the problem of the other. *The International Journal of Psycho-Analysis, 78*(4), 653–666.

Lasch, C. (1979). *The culture of narcissism.* W.W. Norton & Company.

Legerstee, M. (2005). *Infants' sense of people: Precursors to a theory of mind.* Cambridge University Press.

Lenzenweger, M.F., Clarkin, J.F., Kernberg, O.F., & Foelsch, P.A. (2001). The Inventory of Personality Organization: Psychometric properties, factorial composition, and criterion relations with affect, aggressive dyscontrol, psychosis proneness, and self-domains in a nonclinical sample. *Psychological Assessment, 13*(4), 577–591.

Levy, K.N., Clarkin, J.F., Yeomans, F.E., Scott, L.N., & Kernberg, O.F. (2006b). The mechanisms of change in the treatment of borderline personality disorder with transference-focused psychotherapy. *Journal of Clinical Psychology, 62*(4), 481–501. https://doi.org/10.1002/jclp.20239.

Levy, K.N., Meehan, K.B., Kelly, K.M., Reynoso, J.S., Weber,M., Clarkin, J.F., & Kernberg, O.F. (2006a). Change in attachment patterns and reflective function in a randomized control trial of transference-focused psychotherapy for borderline personality disorder. *Journal of Consulting and Clinical Psychology, 74*(6), 1027–1040. https://doi.org/10.1037/0022-006X.74.6.1027.

Levy, K.N., Wasserman, R.H., Meehan, K.B., & Clarkin, J.F. (2008, September 12). *Reflective function as a moderator of dropout in three treatments for BPD* [Paper presentation]. Meeting of the North American Society for Psychotherapy Research (NASPR), New Haven, CT.

Lieberman, J., & Ogas, O. (2015). *Shrinks: The untold story of psychiatry.* Little, Brown.

Linehan, M.M. (1993). *Cognitive-behavioral treatment of borderline personality disorder.* The Guilford Press.

Linehan, M.M., Armstrong, H.E., Suarez, A., Allmon, D., Heard, H.L. (1991). Cognitive-behavioral treatment of chronically parasuicidal borderline patients. *Archives of General Psychiatry, 48*(12), 1060–1064. https://doi.org/10.1001/archpsyc.1991.01810360024003.

Loewald, H. (1960). On the therapeutic action of psycho-analysis. *The International Journal of Psycho-analysis, 41*, 16–33.

López, D., Cuevas, P., Gómez, A., & Mendoza, J. (2004). Psicoterapia focalizada en la transferencia para el trastorno límite de la personalidad. Un estudio con pacientes femininas. *Salud Mental, 27*(4), 44–54.

Mahler, M., Pine, F., & Bergman, A. (1975). *The psychological birth of the human infant.* Basic Books.

Main, M. (1991). Metacognitive knowledge, metacognitive monitoring, and singular (coherent) vs. multiple (incoherent) models of attachment: Findings and directions for future research. In C.M. Parkes, J. Stevenson-Hinde, & P. Marris (Eds.), *Attachment across the life cycle* (pp. 127–159). Tavistock/Routledge.

Main, M., Hesse, E., & Goldwyn, R. (2008). Studying differences in language usage in recounting attachment history: An introduction to the AAI. In H. Steele & M. Steele (Eds.), *Clinical applications of the adult attachment interview* (pp. 31–68). The Guilford Press.

Main, T.F. (1957). The ailment. *British Journal of Medical Psychology, 30*(3), 129–145. https://doi.org/10.1111/j.2044-8341.1957.tb01193.x.

Maxwell, K., & Huprich, S. (2014). Retrospective reports of attachment disruptions, parental abuse and neglect mediate the relationship between pathological narcissism and self-esteem. *Personality and Mental Health, 8*(4), 290–305. https://doi.org/10.1002/pmh.1269.

Mikulincer, M., & Shaver, P.R. (2007). *Attachment in adulthood: Structure, dynamics, and change.* The Guilford Press.

Normandin, L., Ensink, K., Weiner, A., & Kernberg, O.F. (2021). *Transference-focused psychotherapy for adolescents with severe personality disorders.* American Psychiatric Association Publishing.

Northoff, G., Vetter, J., & Böker, H. (2016). Das Selbst und das Gehirn. In H. Böker, P. Hartwich, & G. Northoff (Eds.), *Neuropsychodynamische Psychiatrie* (pp. 129–145). Springer.

Orwell, G. (1950). *1984.* Signet Classic.

Otway, L.J., & Vignoles, V.L. (2006). Narcissism and childhood recollections: A quantitative test of psychoanalytic predictions. *Personality and Social Psychology Bulletin, 32*(1), 104–116. https://doi.org/10.1177/0146167205279907.

Panksepp, J., & Biven, L. (2012). *The archaeology of mind: Neuroevolutionary origins of human emotions.* W.W. Norton & Company.

Paris, J. (2014). Modernity and narcissistic personality disorder. *Personality Disorders: Theory, Research, and Treatment, 5*(2), 220–226. https://doi.org/10.1037/a0028580.

Perez, D.L., Vago, D.R., Pan, H., Root, J., Tuescher, O., Fuchs, B.H., Leung, L., Epstein, J., Cain, N.M., Clarkin, J.F., Lenzenweger, M.F., Kernberg, O.F., Levy, K.N., Silbersweig, D.A., & Stern, E. (2016). Frontolimbic neural circuit changes in emotional processing and inhibitory control associated with clinical improvement following transference-focused psychotherapy in borderline personality disorder. *Psychiatry and Clinical Neurosciences, 70*(1), 51–61. https://doi.org/10.1111/pcn.12357.

Rockland, L.H. (1992). *Supportive therapy for borderline patients: A psychodynamic approach.* The Guilford Press.

Roth, G., & Strüber, N. (2014). *Wie das Gehim die Seele Macht.* Klett-Cotta.

Sharp, C., Wright, A.G.C., Fowler, J.C., Frueh, B.C., Allen, J.G., Oldham, J., & Clark, L.A. (2015). The structure of personality pathology: Both general ('g') and specific ('s') factors? *Journal of Abnormal Psychology, 124*(2), 387–398. https://doi.org/10.1037/abn0000033.

Singer, T. & Hein, G. (2012). Human empathy through the lens of psychology and social neuroscience. In F.B.M. de Waal, & P.F. Ferrari (Eds.), *The primate mind: Built to connect with other minds* (pp. 158–174). Harvard University Press. https://doi.org/10.4159/harvard.9780674062917.

Snyder, T. (2017). *On tyranny: Twenty lessons from the twentieth century.* Tim Duggan Books.

Stanton, A.H., & Schwartz, M.S. (1954). *The mental hospital: A study of institutional participation in psychiatric illness and treatment.* Basic Books.

Steiner, J. (1994). Patient-centered and analyst-centered interpretations: Some implications of containment and countertransference. *Psychoanalytic Inquiry, 14*(3), 406–422. https://doi.org/10.1080/07351699409533994.

Stinson, F.S., Dawson, D.A., Goldstein, R.B., Chou, S.P., Huang, B., Smith, S.M., Ruan, W.J., Pulay, A.J., Saha, T.D., Pickering, R.P., & Grant, B.F. (2008). Prevalence, correlates, disability, and comorbidity of DSM-IV narcissistic personality disorder: Results from the wave 2 national epidemiologic survey on alcohol and related conditions. *The Journal of Clinical Psychiatry, 69*(7), 1033–1045. https://doi.org/10.4088/jcp.v69n0701.

Tronick, E.Z. (1998). Dyadically expanded states of consciousness and the process of therapeutic change. *Infant Mental Health Journal, 19*(3), 290–299. https://doi.org/10.1002/(SICI)1097-0355(199823)19:3<290::AID-IMHJ4>3.0.CO;2-Q.

Tronick, E.Z. (2007). *The neurobehavioral and social-emotional development of infants and children.* W.W. Norton & Company.

Trull, T.J., Jahng, S., Tomko, R.L., Wood, P.K., & Sher, K.J. (2010). Revised NESARC personality disorder diagnoses: Gender, prevalence, and comorbidity with substance dependence disorders. *Journal of Personality Disorders, 24*(4), 412–426. https://doi.org/10.1521/pedi.2010.24.4.412.

Turquet, P. (1975). Threats to identity in the large group. In L. Kreeger (Ed.), *The large group: Dynamics and therapy* (pp. 87–144). Routledge.

Twenge, J.M., Konrath, S., Foster, J.D., Campbell, W.K., & Bushman, B.J. (2008). Egos inflating over time: A cross-temporal meta-analysis of the Narcissistic Personality Inventory. *Journal of Personality, 76*(4), 875–902. https://doi.org/10.1111/j.1467-6494.2008.00507.x.

Vaillant, G.E. (1994). Ego mechanisms of defense and personality psychopathology. *Journal of Abnormal Psychology, 103*(1), 44–50. https://doi.org/10.1037//0021-843x.103.1.44.

Wallerstein, R.S., Luborsky, L., Robbins, L.L., & Sargent, H.D. (1956). The psycho-therapy research project of the Menninger foundation: Rationale, method, and sample use. *Bulletin of the Menninger Clinic, 20*(5), 221–278.

Weiner, A., Biberdzic, M., Bates, J., Sowislo, J. Ensink, K., Clarkin, A., Normandin, L., & Clarkin, J.F. (2023). *STIPO-R for adolescents*. Unpublished manuscript.

World Health Organization (2019). *International statistical classification of diseases and related health problems* (11th ed. revision). https://icd.who.int/browse11

Yeomans, F.E., Clarkin, J.F., & Kernberg, O.F. (2015). *Transference-focused psychotherapy for borderline personality disorder: A clinical guide*. American Psychiatric Association Publishing.

Yeomans, F.E., Selzer, M.A., & Clarkin, J.F. (1992). *Treating the borderline patient: A contract-based approach*. Basic Books.

Young, S.M. & Pinsky, D. (2006). Narcissism and celebrity. *Journal of Research in Personality, 40*(5), 463–471. https://doi.org/10.1016/j.jrp.2006.05.005.

Index

Note: **Bold** page numbers refer to tables and page numbers followed by "n" denote endnotes.

deviations from neutrality
50–51; diagnostic sessions 43;
emotional intensity 44; extended
41; functions 43; interpretative
process 58–59; interpretive
process 52–53; manual
justification 41–42; narcissistic
personality 41; neutrality 57;
NPD 54–56; patient's history
45; psychoanalytic work 56–57;
research 64; respective roles of
patients 44; role of therapist 44;
strategies 46–47; tactics 47–48;
technical neutrality 49–50;

techniques 48–49; therapist's
position 45; transference analysis
53–54, 59–60; unconscious
motivations 42
Turquet, P. 99
Twenge, J.M. 96–98

Van der Waals, H. 5
video recordings 67
Vienna-Munich RCT 72
virtual sexual engagements 87

Wallerstein, R. 3, 4, 62
Will, O. 3

Printed and bound by CPI Group (UK) Ltd, Croydon, CR0 4YY

18/07/2024

01019570-0005